M000033348

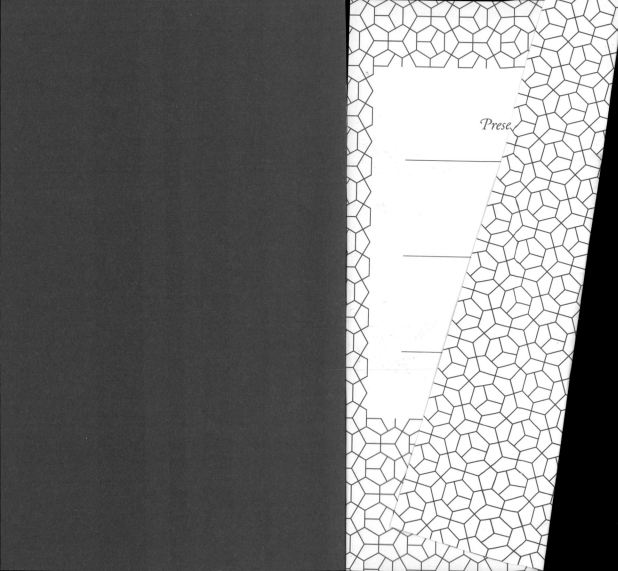

Prese

THE ONE YEAR®

BOOK OF BEST-LOVED BIBLE VERSES

DEVOTIONAL

LEN WOODS

TYNDALE
MOMENTUM®

*The nonfiction imprint of
Tyndale House Publishers, Inc.*

Visit Tyndale online at www.tyndale.com.

Visit Tyndale Momentum online at www.tyndalemomentum.com.

TYNDALE, Tyndale Momentum, Tyndale's quill logo, *The One Year,* and *One Year* are registered trademarks of Tyndale House Publishers, Inc. The Tyndale Momentum logo and The One Year logo are trademarks of Tyndale House Publishers, Inc. Tyndale Momentum is the nonfiction imprint of Tyndale House Publishers, Inc., Carol Stream, Illinois.

The One Year® Book of Best-Loved Bible Verses

Designed by Nicole Grimes (cover) and Dean H. Renninger (interior)

Edited by Ellen Richard Vosburg

Produced with the assistance of Hudson Bible (www.HudsonBible.com). Project staff includes Christopher D. Hudson, Len Woods, and Mary Larsen.

For information about special discounts for bulk purchases, please contact Tyndale House Publishers at csresponse@tyndale.com, or call 1-800-323-9400.

ISBN 978-1-4964-2300-9

Printed in China

24	23	22	21	20	19	18
7	6	5	4	3	2	1

INTRODUCTION

At the bottom of a dusty trunk, you find a Bible that is scuffed and scarred, held together by dried-out rubber bands and old, yellowed tape. Why does it look like it's been through a war or two? Because it has been!

You gently open the crumbling cover. You carefully examine the tattered text. Here is what you discover: from beginning to end are verses—some familiar, some not—that have been underlined, starred, highlighted. Many are accompanied by tiny cursive notes in the nearest margin.

These are someone's favorite passages, of course.

In a life full of joy and grief, faith and doubt, there are particular passages of Scripture that have been the go-to verses for many across the long history of the church. They are the divine assurances and reminders that have often served as eternal anchors and ropes of hope in a stormy, scary world. Here is a treasury of holy messages—things *always* true even when they don't *seem* true.

In these pages I've collected a year's worth of such verses for you. Understand this: these 365 best-loved Bible verses certainly aren't more inspired than the rest of Scripture. But many report how these verses seem to jump off the page and how perfectly they capture the human experience. Memorable, profound, endlessly reassuring—no wonder people keep highlighting and underlining them (and posting them on social media)!

So—from the poetry of David and the wisdom of Solomon to the teachings of Jesus and the apostles—here are the verses that millions of Christians through the ages have found most inspiring, encouraging, comforting, and life changing.

Through his Word, God reveals himself to seekers. As you seek, my prayer is that you will be as blessed by these passages as all those who have gone before you.

OUR HEART'S DESIRE

*Take delight in the LORD, and he will
give you your heart's desires.*

PSALM 37:4

This beloved verse doesn't mean that God gives us anything we ask for. What wise, responsible father does that?

Delighting in God means enjoying him, finding great pleasure and satisfaction in him. As we do this, we come to see that we were made by God and for him. And we realize our deepest longing is for *him*, not for any earthly blessings he might give.

If your desires are jumbled, consider the honest prayer of an old saint, Teresa of Avila: "Oh God, I don't love you, I don't even want to love you, but I want to want to love you."

*Even if he does not bring you the answer you want,
he will bring you himself. And maybe at the secret heart
of all our prayers that is what we are really praying for.*

FREDERICK BUECHNER

TRUSTWORTHY INSPIRATION

All Scripture is inspired by God and is useful to teach us what is true and to make us realize what is wrong in our lives. It corrects us when we are wrong and teaches us to do what is right.

2 TIMOTHY 3:16

People speak of books that *inspire*, but the Bible claims to *be inspired*. *Inspiration* means that God's Spirit superintended the human authors so that they accurately conveyed God's revelation to the world through their own unique writing styles and personalities.

Since God speaks only truth, his Word can be trusted. Let it be a mirror today, showing you where your life is flawed. Let it be your toolbox, helping you repair what's broken. Let it be your GPS, guiding you in the right way.

Don't believe everything you think. You cannot be trusted to tell yourself the truth. Stay in The Word.

JERRY BRIDGES

DOING THE WORD

Don't just listen to God's word.
You must do what it says.

JAMES 1:22

A group of Christians held a Bible study on the topic of prayer. Each Tuesday they spent two hours learning about prayer. But, except for a quick "closing prayer" each week, they didn't do any praying!

In the information age, it's easy to fall into the information trap. We can gorge on great books and podcasts, stuff our heads full of theological truth—and remain essentially unchanged.

This isn't what the Christian life is meant to be. Following Jesus is not a thought experiment. It's obeying what God has said. Every time we close the Bible, we need to ask: *How will I live differently?*

The Bible was not written to satisfy your curiosity;
it was written to transform your life.

HOWARD HENDRICKS

GOD IS SPEAKING

The heavens proclaim the glory of God. The skies display his craftsmanship. Day after day they continue to speak; night after night they make him known.

PSALM 19:1-2

Perhaps you know someone who has heard the audible voice of God. Maybe you think, *How come I've never heard God speak like that?*

God speaks in a host of ways. We can hear his voice throughout his Word, and his voice can seem especially clear as we encounter Jesus within the pages of the Word. If you are eager to hear from God, the Gospels are a great place to start.

The psalmist reminds us today that God also speaks through creation, which makes him known. Even in life's mundane moments, the Holy Spirit is whispering. So pay attention, or as Jesus put it, "Anyone with ears to hear should listen and understand!" (Matthew 11:15).

[God] is by His nature continuously articulate. He fills the world with His speaking Voice.

A. W. TOZER

BIG GOD,
LITTLE PROBLEMS

*Who else has held the oceans in his hand? Who has measured
off the heavens with his fingers? Who else knows the weight of
the earth or has weighed the mountains and hills on a scale?*

ISAIAH 40:12

Someone once quipped, "Little god, big problems. Big
God, little problems." However simplistic that saying
might be, it is nevertheless true. Seeing the magnitude
of our Maker puts everything else in right perspective.

In describing the immensity of God, Isaiah imagined
the Almighty scooping the Pacific and Atlantic Oceans
into one hand while palming the Milky Way with the
other. Then he described God placing the Himalayas and
Rockies on a scale.

Are you getting the picture? God is infinite and limitless. This means he's plenty big enough for whatever
you're up against.

*Happy the soul that has been awed
by a view of God's majesty.*

A. W. PINK

HIDDEN REALITIES

We live by believing and not by seeing.
2 CORINTHIANS 5:7

Most people live according to what they can *see*. For example, you may survey your life and conclude, *I have zero job prospects, no friends, and no money to pay my bills. I'm ruined!*

The problem with this mind-set is that it's limited by space and time. It forgets that reality transcends what is visible here and now. It neglects the following twin truths: (1) At every moment, God is orchestrating and coordinating a trillion details. (2) We can see precious little of all God is doing.

Since you don't know about that phone call you'll be getting next Friday or the surprise that awaits you tomorrow at 9:32 a.m., opt to live by faith, not by what you can or cannot see.

Some things have to be believed to be seen.
RALPH HODGSON

NO OTHER GODS

*Dear children, keep away from anything that
might take God's place in your hearts.*

1 JOHN 5:21

Ancient cultures weren't the only ones susceptible to idolatry.

An idol is anything other than God that we depend on to save us or give us meaning. An idol is often a *good* thing—marriage, an ability, a career, children, financial success—that we treat as an *ultimate* thing. We wrap our hearts around it and think, *Without this, my life's not worth living.*

This is the essence of sin—giving our hearts to anything but God. Are there things in your life that receive more attention, affection, and adoration from you than God receives?

The human mind is, so to speak, a perpetual forge of idols.
JOHN CALVIN

DIVINE LOVE AFFAIR

Listen, O Israel! The LORD is our God, the LORD alone. And you must love the LORD your God with all your heart, all your soul, and all your strength.

DEUTERONOMY 6:4-5

A "just married" couple practically skipping up the aisle. An ardent advocate championing a noble cause. A dedicated teacher rising before the sun. Don't you love to see people who have given their hearts fully to someone or something? Such people are tireless, committed, and wildly unpredictable. They take risks and make beautiful sacrifices.

Today's beloved passage urges us not to settle for a humdrum faith. If you feel you're just going through the spiritual motions today, ask God to jump-start your heart. Tell him you want to return to your "first love" (see Revelation 2:4). Then ask an older, wiser believer how to put a little spice back in your faith.

Let your religion be less of a theory and more of a love affair.

G. K. CHESTERTON

SURE THING

I have written this to you who believe in the name of the Son of God, so that you may know you have eternal life.

1 JOHN 5:13

Surveys show that many church attenders aren't sure they "have eternal life." When asked about heaven, they say things like, "I *hope* I'm going." Others are less sure: "I guess I'll find out when I die."

God doesn't want us in the dark about something as important as eternal life. He wants us to know now. What's more, he reveals how we can be sure.

Eternal life is a gift (see 1 John 5:11). It's not something we earn by good behavior. We receive this gift by believing in who Jesus is and trusting what he did. That's it. That's how you can "know you have eternal life."

Assurance is a fruit that grows out of the root of faith.
STEPHEN CHARNOCK

GOD-FEARING?

*Come, my children, and listen to me, and
I will teach you to fear the LORD.*

PSALM 34:11

Over and over in the Bible, we see examples of people who encounter the shattering holiness of God's physical presence and fall to the ground in abject terror. This is "the fear of the LORD"—a raw awe that rocks you to your core.

For believers, "the fear of the LORD" means deep reverence. We glimpse God's majesty, or we are rocked by his goodness. Suddenly we find ourselves breathless, speechless, shaking our heads in awe. Trembling with humility, we wonder, *How could a great God like this love someone like me?* Something in us shifts. We leave the encounter changed for the better.

The psalmist today encourages us to learn to fear the Lord. Ask the Lord right now to teach you to have a deep reverence for him.

We fear men so much, because we fear God so little.
WILLIAM GURNALL

WANTED: SINNERS

This is a trustworthy saying, and everyone should accept it: "Christ Jesus came into the world to save sinners"—and I am the worst of them all.

1 TIMOTHY 1:15

Before the Roman Empire set out to destroy the church, a young, zealous Pharisee thought he was defending the faith by murdering those who were actually most faithful to God. This prideful, hateful man was named Saul, and he was hell-bent on destroying the Christian faith.

Then the hunter became the hunted. The risen Christ ambushed Saul. Jesus blinded him to open his eyes, knocked him in the dirt to make him clean, and gave him a new life and a new calling.

If we're looking for an illustration of grace, we can't do better than Saul (later known as Paul). The fact that God would not only choose but also use somebody like him means that God can certainly use us.

I have been all things unholy. If God can work through me, He can work through anyone.

ATTRIBUTED TO FRANCIS OF ASSISI

HOW TO MAKE IT TO THE NEXT ROUND

God saved you by his grace when you believed. And you can't take credit for this; it is a gift from God.

EPHESIANS 2:8

Religion can feel a lot like a reality TV talent show: "Do your best. Try to impress the Judge. See if you can do well enough to make it to the next round."

The gospel of Jesus says, "You'll never be good enough. However, if you'll admit that truth, abandon your act, and let Jesus include you in *his* act, you'll win the big prize."

This imperfect illustration makes a key point about the gospel: divine approval and blessing have nothing to do with us and everything to do with Jesus.

Ask people what they must do to get to heaven and most reply, "Be good." Jesus' stories contradict that answer. All we must do is cry, "Help!"

PHILIP YANCEY

THE CART
AFTER THE HORSE

We are God's masterpiece. He has created us
anew in Christ Jesus, so we can do the good
things he planned for us long ago.

EPHESIANS 2:10

Religious legalism claims, "Do good works so that God will accept you." The gospel flips this erroneous notion on its head, saying, "Because God *has* accepted you in Christ, do good works."

Beware of putting the cart before the horse. Grace is "undeserved favor." Salvation is a gift—not a payment for services rendered. How do we receive this astonishing gift of forgiveness and new life? We accept it by faith in Jesus (see Ephesians 2:8-9).

After we've been made new by Christ, *then* we can rightly engage in new behaviors for Christ.

Abhor all idea of being saved by good works, but O,
be as full of good works as if you were to be saved by them!

CHARLES H. SPURGEON

COMING INTO THE LIGHT

People who conceal their sins will not prosper, but if they confess and turn from them, they will receive mercy.

PROVERBS 28:13

Do something wrong and watch the devil pounce. The "father of lies" (John 8:44) will first condemn. Next he'll hiss, "Keep it hidden! If anyone finds out, your life will be over!"

The truth is just the opposite. It's by coming into the light and coming clean that we experience forgiveness and relief. That's how we are healed.

Don't believe the enemy's lie. It's hiding (i.e., *not* being honest) that keeps us sick. Acknowledging our sin might be humbling, but it's the only way to get well.

To confess your sins to God is not to tell him anything he doesn't already know. Until you confess them, however, they are the abyss between you. When you confess them, they become the Golden Gate Bridge.

FREDERICK BUECHNER

LOOK UNDER THE HOOD

*A good person produces good things from the treasury
of a good heart, and an evil person produces evil
things from the treasury of an evil heart.*

MATTHEW 12:35

When your vehicle starts acting up, it's time to head to
the nearest car wash, right? Wrong. Substantive, internal
problems aren't fixed by superficial, external solutions.

As a car's performance depends on its engine, so
our behavior depends on our hearts. Whatever is in our
hearts emerges on the surface of our lives. Those filled
with compassion engage in caring acts. Those filled with
anger lash out at those around them.

The next time you're perplexed or embarrassed by
a sinful reaction, examine your heart. Ask, "Lord, what
wrongly held belief or misplaced love is driving my
behavior?" Remember: everything starts with the heart.

*O holy Spirit, Love of God, infuse Thy grace, and descend
plentifully into my heart; enlighten the dark corners of this
neglected dwelling, and scatter there Thy cheerful beams.*

AUGUSTINE OF HIPPO

DON'T FORGET TO REMEMBER

*Watch out! Be careful never to forget what you yourself
have seen. Do not let these memories escape from
your mind as long as you live! And be sure to pass
them on to your children and grandchildren.*

DEUTERONOMY 4:9

The biblical emphasis on *remembering* is due to our human problem of *forgetting*.

Sin produces a deadly kind of "spiritual dementia" in our hearts. This is why God gave the Israelites the Passover Feast by which to remember their deliverance from Egypt. This is why there are only about ten major themes in the Bible, and God just keeps repeating them over and over.

Take some time today to think back on your spiritual history. Then tell the stories of God's faithfulness to your friends and family. This is how we remember to remember.

*Christians are "memorial people" because the whole
of our faith depends upon remembering.*

JON BLOOM

NO MORE DULL PEOPLE

As iron sharpens iron, so a friend sharpens a friend.

PROVERBS 27:17

Ancient craftsmen sharpened their tools by striking them repeatedly against each other. Today, we rub a metal file across a tool's edge. This process generates noise, friction, heat—sometimes even sparks! The end result is a sharp chisel, a more useful machete, a knife that actually cuts.

Solomon used this practice to illustrate what happens when friends butt heads. Healthy conflict isn't fun, but if we're humble enough to listen and learn from others, our rough edges gradually get knocked away.

Who are you allowing to knock up against the rough edges of your life to make you better?

Many of us have never invited someone else to be a Truth-Teller in our lives for the same reason we don't get on a scale: We are afraid of what we might find out.

JOHN ORTBERG

A PARABLE ABOUT OBEDIENCE

My sheep listen to my voice; I know them, and they follow me.

JOHN 10:27

A man went to lunch with some business associates. After ordering, he mumbled an offensive comment about the server, only to realize she was standing *right behind him*!

More than embarrassment, the man felt an over-powering sense of conviction. *Go apologize!* an internal voice insisted. It wasn't audible, but it was deafening. When the server brought their checks, the man couldn't even bring himself to make eye contact.

When the Holy Spirit speaks to you, listen; when he convicts, obey.

God desires the least degree of obedience and submissiveness more than all those services you think of rendering him.

JOHN OF THE CROSS

GREAT ENEMY, GREATER SAVIOR

Stay alert! Watch out for your great enemy,
the devil. He prowls around like a roaring
lion, looking for someone to devour.

1 PETER 5:8

C. S. Lewis observed that most people either obsess over the idea of Satan or smirk at such a quaint superstition.

This verse reminds us the devil is 100 percent real. Peter calls him our "great enemy" and describes his vicious behavior—prowling about, hoping to have some poor, unsuspecting soul for lunch.

Should we panic? No! Satan is no match for our Savior. But we should "stay alert." How are you carefully watching out for devilish schemes in your life?

The devil can handle me—he's got judo I never heard
of. But he can't handle the One to whom I'm joined;
he can't handle the One to whom I'm united; he can't
handle the One whose nature dwells in my nature.

A. W. TOZER

CHANGING FOR BETTER (OR WORSE)

*Don't copy the behavior and customs of this world, but
let God transform you into a new person by changing
the way you think. Then you will learn to know God's
will for you, which is good and pleasing and perfect.*

ROMANS 12:2

As God's children, we find within us the desire to know
and follow Jesus. But as citizens of an alluring world, we
also feel the tremendous tug of culture. Do you feel that
clash of kingdoms in your own heart?

Paul says we will change—one way or the other. Our
lives will reflect either the character of Jesus or society's
values. Only the power of the Word can thwart the pull
of the world.

*Turn your eyes upon Jesus, look full in His wonderful
face, and the things of earth will grow strangely
dim, in the light of His glory and grace.*

HELEN LEMMEL

THE STUFF OF HEAVEN

Think about the things of heaven, not the things of earth.

COLOSSIANS 3:2

Turn off the alarm, drink some coffee, hit the gym, fight traffic, endure meetings, answer phone calls, rewrite the report, fight traffic again, pay bills, watch TV, set the alarm, then collapse in exhaustion so you can do it all again tomorrow.

If we're not careful, we can turn into automatons. We can buy into a frantic lifestyle that is more reflexive than reflective. Soon the faint, beautiful call of the "Not yet" is drowned out by the blaring call of the superficial "Now!" Laser-focused on the urgent, we miss the important.

The Bible is clear: reality transcends what we experience with our physical senses. Today, remember this: there's more to this life than this life.

All that is not eternal is eternally out of date.

C. S. LEWIS

AMAGING JESUS

When Jesus heard this, he was amazed. Turning to those who were following him, he said, "I tell you the truth, I haven't seen faith like this in all Israel!"

MATTHEW 8:10

People applaud certain kinds of feats as the pinnacle of human achievement—like scaling Mount Everest or writing a *New York Times* bestseller. But Jesus is interested in something else.

When a Roman army officer approached Jesus on behalf of his sick servant, his faith left the Son of God amazed. Jesus actually gushed about the man to everyone within earshot! Contrast this with another time Jesus was said to be amazed—when the people in his own hometown had zero faith in him (see Mark 6:6).

As noteworthy as human accomplishment can be, it's even more impressive to cultivate the kind of faith that Jesus finds amazing.

You do not need a great faith, but faith in a great God.
HUDSON TAYLOR

NO ACCIDENT

In the beginning God created the heavens and the earth.

GENESIS 1:1

Some Christians believe the cosmos is young. Others think that biblical revelation allows for—and scientific evidence points to—an older earth.

On this biblical fact, however, there is no disagreement: "God created."

Christians believe that the world didn't just "happen" as the result of a cosmic accident. The first chapters of Genesis tell us that a wise and good Creator made the universe and everything in it.

Today as you look in the mirror or watch birds dig for worms or listen to a loved one tell about their day, remember Genesis 1:1 and take a few moments to praise your Maker. We are walking, talking wonders, living inside a cosmic miracle.

What can be more foolish than to think that all this rare fabric of heaven and earth could come by chance, when all the skill of art is not able to make an oyster!

JEREMY TAYLOR

UNDER CONSTRUCTION

*I am certain that God, who began the good work
within you, will continue his work until it is finally
finished on the day when Christ Jesus returns.*

PHILIPPIANS 1:6

When asked about salvation, Christians should answer, "Yes, I *have been* saved. And, what's more, I *am being* saved."

Salvation in the fullest sense includes both a finished aspect (being spared the penalty of sin—justification) and a continuing aspect (being delivered from the power of sin—sanctification).

According to Paul in this popular verse, God is working steadily in us to make us like Jesus. The project's completion date? The glorious day we come face to face with him.

What specific step will you take today to cooperate with God's good work for your life?

*If God should justify a people and not sanctify them,
he should justify a people whom he could not glorify.*

THOMAS WATSON

WHAT WE HATE

---

*I don't really understand myself, for I want to do what
is right, but I don't do it. Instead, I do what I hate.*

ROMANS 7:15

It's 11:34 p.m. and *she* can't sleep because of the fierce
fight she had with her daughter over homework. So
much for all that earnest prayer beforehand.

Meanwhile, *he's* wide awake too, the quilt covering
him like so much guilt. Tonight he clicked his way to a
website he swore he was done visiting. *Why?* he laments
silently. *Why do I keep going there?*

Though placing our faith in Christ gives us a new
nature that desires to please God, Paul reminds us that
Christians still battle old thought patterns and habits.
Following Jesus is learning how to live out of our new,
true identity by relying on the Word of God, the Spirit
of God, and the people of God.

Nothing is easier than sinning.
MARTIN LUTHER

WORLDLY LOVE

Do not love this world nor the things it offers you, for when you love the world, you do not have the love of the Father in you.

1 JOHN 2:15

John 3:16 speaks of God's love for the world. Ephesians 5:1 tells believers to be imitators of God. Why then does John forbid Christians from loving the world?

God's love for the world seeks to transform. The love John condemns here is different. It's a conforming love. Instead of confronting the status quo, it accepts and embraces the spirit and customs of the age.

John is saying that when citizens of heaven find themselves comfortably at home in a fallen world, something is terribly wrong.

There is a common worldly kind of Christianity in this day, which many have; a cheap Christianity which offends nobody, which requires no sacrifice, which costs nothing and is worth nothing!

J. C. RYLE

TEARS IN A BOTTLE

---

*You keep track of all my sorrows. You have collected all my
tears in your bottle. You have recorded each one in your book.*

PSALM 56:8

If you're hurting today, be assured of this: your grief does
not escape God's notice. The Almighty sees your sorrow
and catalogs your pain. He is collecting all your tears.

"That's just poetic language!" some protest. Perhaps.
But the Bible assures us that God is in the process of
restoring all things. One day he will do away with crying
itself (see Revelation 21:4).

Maybe on that great day we'll stand with God and
watch him empty our tears into an ocean of infinite joy.
For every drop of grief we've felt on earth, he will give us
20,000 leagues of gladness in heaven.

Earth has no sorrow that heaven cannot heal.

THOMAS MOORE

SPIRITUAL CHECKUP TIME?

Search me, O God, and know my heart; test me and know my anxious thoughts. Point out anything in me that offends you, and lead me along the path of everlasting life.

PSALM 139:23-24

You've got a pain that won't go away. You see your doctor, and what follows is a lot of poking, prodding, and medical testing. Hopefully, you receive a clear diagnosis and treatment.

In Psalm 139, David undergoes a comparable spiritual checkup. After remembering God's all-knowing and ever-present nature, David asks his Maker to examine his heart—in effect, to do an MRI on his soul.

Who doesn't need an appointment with the Great Physician on a regular basis—a thorough examination for any signs of spiritual sickness, an accurate diagnosis of a problem, a surefire prescription for health?

Will you let God search your heart today?

We must lay before [God] what is in us, not what ought to be in us.

C. S. LEWIS

JOB DESCRIPTION

"The time promised by God has come at last!"
[Jesus] announced. "The Kingdom of God is near!
Repent of your sins and believe the Good News!"

MARK 1:15

Jesus began his public ministry with two commands—
Repent and *believe the Good News.*

The call to *repent* causes the most indigestion. Contrary to popular belief, repentance isn't "getting a spiritual whooping." It's receiving a gracious invitation to come into the light and adjust our lives accordingly. Repentance is more *epiphany* than *emotion.* But it often includes tears of regret. It always means rethinking and restructuring one's life.

According to Jesus, repenting and believing are how we begin a relationship with God. They are also how we walk with him each day for the rest of our lives. What attitude or action do you need to repent of today?

The Christian who has stopped
repenting has stopped growing.

A. W. PINK

WHERE LIFE BEGINS

Guard your heart above all else,
for it determines the course of your life.

PROVERBS 4:23

In the Bible, the heart isn't simply the touchy-feely part of one's personhood. It's also where we think and reason, choose and obey. In short, the heart is the command center of our lives.

No wonder this beloved verse urges us to watch over our hearts with the utmost diligence. The kind of lives we live depends on the kind of hearts we have. If our hearts aren't right, nothing else about our lives will be either.

What does the current direction of your life say about the current condition of your heart? Joy and passion for God or disobedience and spiritual apathy—everything starts in the heart.

You must keep all earthly treasures out of your heart, and
let Christ be your treasure, and let him have your heart.

CHARLES H. SPURGEON

DOUBTING BELIEVERS

*The father instantly cried out, "I do believe,
but help me overcome my unbelief!"*

MARK 9:24

Every parent knows the panic of having a child in trouble. And every honest believer is familiar with that murky no-man's-land somewhere between faith and doubt.

This oft-quoted verse is exclaimed by a father who faced both trials at once. His child and his faith were both on life support. *I can't honestly say I trust you deeply, Lord,* he seems to be confessing, *but I want to. Will you help me?*

This is the spiritual life in a nutshell. We begin the journey with Christ by faith. But along the way, difficulties come and doubts creep in.

What has you questioning God's power or wisdom today? Call on him to revive your faith.

*If you don't have doubts you're either kidding
yourself or asleep. Doubts are the ants-in-the-
pants of faith. They keep it alive and moving.*

FREDERICK BUECHNER

TIME FLIES

---

*Teach us to realize the brevity of life, so
that we may grow in wisdom.*

PSALM 90:12

Everyone speaks of how time flies. But precious few adjust their lives to account for this reality.

Scripture says that God has allotted each of us a precise number of days (Psalm 139:16). This number is set by him. It's fixed. We don't get one day more. We won't get one day less. Remembering this keeps us from presuming about the future. Perhaps you have ten thousand tomorrows left. Or you might just have two. Only God knows.

Don't wait for a tragedy or a dark diagnosis to begin living intentionally. Live today in light of eternity. Live for the glory of God and the good of the world.

*Desire that your life count for something great! Long
for your life to have eternal significance. Want this!
Don't coast through life without a passion.*

JOHN PIPER

WHERE'S YOUR FAITH?

Faith shows the reality of what we hope for;
it is the evidence of things we cannot see.

HEBREWS 11:1

At the bistro on the corner, everyone's full of faith. An agnostic businessman clearly believes his soup du jour (prepared by someone he's never seen) is safe to eat. His irreligious waitress believes she'll get a nice tip if she takes good care of him and his well-to-do party of six.

Meanwhile, the nervous mom in the corner is trusting God for a good conversation with the grown daughter she hasn't seen in over a year.

See, it's really not a question of *if* we believe—everybody believes *something*. The real question is this: In *what* or in *whom* do we trust? And, even more importantly, is our ultimate faith in Christ?

Faith is the "yes" of the heart, a conviction
on which one stakes one's life.
MARTIN LUTHER

REVIVAL TIME?

If my people who are called by my name will humble
themselves and pray and seek my face and turn from
their wicked ways, I will hear from heaven and
will forgive their sins and restore their land.

2 CHRONICLES 7:14

Many believers see this oft-quoted verse as a surefire formula for contemporary revival. Others disagree, arguing this promise was given uniquely to the nation of Israel.

This much is clear: God wants us to be humble (James 4:6), to pray faithfully (1 Timothy 2:1-2), to seek him (Hebrews 11:6), and to be holy (1 Peter 1:15). All those pursuits honor God. Whether such things spark a national spiritual awakening is entirely up to him. But every revival has to start somewhere. Why not in your heart?

There has never been a spiritual awakening in any
country or locality that did not begin in united prayer.

A. T. PIERSON

SPIRITUAL TERRORISM

We are not fighting against flesh-and-blood enemies,
but against evil rulers and authorities of the unseen
world, against mighty powers in this dark world,
and against evil spirits in the heavenly places.

EPHESIANS 6:12

You discover a neighbor two doors down is planning a violent attack at a nearby sports stadium. Do you: (a) binge watch that new series on Netflix; (b) take a nap; (c) daydream about retirement; or (d) go into emergency mode?

Obviously, no sane person would ignore such a life-and-death threat. So why do we yawn at verses like the one above?

According to the Bible, we live in a world at war spiritually. Whether we sense it or not, we are surrounded by invisible forces that want to destroy us. Recognizing the reality of spiritual warfare is step one in winning the fight.

Spiritual Christians have a life of labor; they look upon
the world not as a playground but as a battleground.

A. W. TOZER

DON'T JUST SIT THERE

An open rebuke is better than hidden love! Wounds from a sincere friend are better than many kisses from an enemy.

PROVERBS 27:5-6

Someone you love is messing up. You feel compelled to speak up. But the voices of culture are deafening: "Be tolerant!" "Who are *you* to judge?"

You could do what most do—look the other way and say nothing. But the Lord calls his followers to confront one another in love.

Few people take correction well, but don't allow the fear of a negative response to keep you from speaking up when you discern that it's the right thing to do. It's better to engage with grace and truth than watch fellow Christians foolishly ruin their lives.

Nothing can be more cruel than that leniency which abandons others to their sin. Nothing can be more compassionate than that severe reprimand which calls another Christian in one's community back from the path of sin.

DIETRICH BONHOEFFER

ENDURING LOVE

Give thanks to the LORD, for he is good!
His faithful love endures forever.

PSALM 136:1

Your child incessantly calls your name. Advertisers on TV and radio repeat their phone numbers again and again. What's with all the repetition? The child wants our attention. The others want their information to stick with us so we buy their products.

In Psalm 136, the psalmist repeats "[God's] faithful love endures forever"—twenty-six times! Like a drumbeat, this steady refrain highlights God's undying commitment to his people. This repetition reminds us that his love for us will never, ever cease.

Here's a challenge to spend a few minutes reviewing your life today. Pause and give thanks (repeatedly!) for specific instances of God's faithful love.

The same everlasting Father who cares for you today will
take care of you then and every day. . . . Be at peace, then,
and put aside all anxious thoughts and imagination.

ST. FRANCIS DE SALES

FRET NOT!

Give all your worries and cares to God, for he cares about you.

1 PETER 5:7

A husband gently chides his fretful wife: "Honey, don't you realize that 95 percent of the stuff you worry about *never* happens?" She furrows her brow for a moment, then nods in smug satisfaction. "See, worrying *works*!"

Worry whispers, "Let's pretend God doesn't exist and play the 'what if' game." Worrying is simply God-less meditation on worst-case scenarios. What a dead end!

Followers of Jesus can cultivate a different habit. Instead of dismissing God from the picture, we invite him into every situation. We remember he is Savior, Lord, Sustainer, and Keeper. Because he's always on duty, we don't have to fret.

Have courage for the great sorrows of life and patience for the small ones; and when you have laboriously accomplished your daily task, go to sleep in peace. God is awake.

VICTOR HUGO

THAT'S NOT GOD'S VOICE

Now there is no condemnation for those
who belong to Christ Jesus.

ROMANS 8:1

Every Christian is familiar with the drill. You sin in some grievous way. Almost immediately you hear it—that voice of withering criticism. Dripping with disgust, it delights in dishing up shame and heaping on scorn.

Guess what? That's not God's voice. That's the enemy, the one the Bible calls the "accuser" of believers (Revelation 12:10).

The gospel assures us that because Jesus took all the condemnation we sinners deserved, we can't justly be accused anymore. In fact, it's even better: we not only escape condemnation but also get the commendation Jesus deserves!

Refuse to listen to the devil's false accusations.

No condemnation now I dread; Jesus, and all
in Him, is mine! Alive in Him, my living Head,
and clothed in righteousness Divine.

CHARLES WESLEY

A SONG OF PEACE

*You will keep in perfect peace all who trust in
you, all whose thoughts are fixed on you!*

ISAIAH 26:3

In his ancient song about a future era of unparalleled blessing, Isaiah revealed how to find peace today.

Resist the powerful urge to focus on your negative circumstances. Force your mind instead to look to God. Thoughts fixed on God are thoughts that lean against, rest upon, and are supported by divine truth.

So if you are facing a senseless, painful situation in your life right now, you could anxiously fix your thoughts on its negative implications. Or you can remember—and trust—that your God is good, wise, powerful, and in control. Not much of a choice, is it?

*[The Christian] believes [God] to be too wise
to err and too good to be unkind; he trusts him
where he cannot trace him, looks up to him in the
darkest hour, and believes that all is well.*

CHARLES H. SPURGEON

WHAT KIDS TEACH US

Let the children come to me. Don't stop them! For the Kingdom of God belongs to those who are like these children.

LUKE 18:16

We can learn a lot from a class of three-year-olds. Though they're highly dependent (kids aren't terribly bothered by that fact), they trust. Look how confidently they leap into the arms of a trusted adult.

They live almost entirely in the moment. They're careless in the best sense of the word. They aren't sinless, but they possess a kind of innocence. They haven't yet learned how to play mind games or wear masks. What you see is what you get.

It's interesting that Jesus would use children to illustrate how he wants his adult followers to live. So when it comes to the spiritual life, are you more like a trusting child or a cynical, independent adult?

If we love Christ much, surely we shall trust Him much.

THOMAS BROOKS

FEBRUARY 11

LOVING LIKE JESUS

Love is patient and kind. Love is not jealous or
boastful or proud or rude. It does not demand its
own way. It is not irritable, and it keeps no record
of being wronged. It does not rejoice about injustice
but rejoices whenever the truth wins out.

1 CORINTHIANS 13:4-6

As the minister reads this famous passage over the couple
at the altar—his words a sort of prayer—the cynic smirks,
thinking of the meaningless pep talks his high school
coach used to give before impossible games.

Left to ourselves, such love *is* impossible, of course.
The good news is that Christ loves this way. And he will
love this way *through us* if we'll let him.

When Christ comes into your life and you become a
Christian, God gives you the resources to be a different kind
of person. . . . He provides you with a new kind of love.

BILL BRIGHT

NEVER SAY DIE

Love never gives up, never loses faith, is always hopeful,
and endures through every circumstance.

1 CORINTHIANS 13:7

"We fell madly in love, but after a while our love died." To hear some people tell it, love is a virus you catch, a whim you indulge, a fad you decide to explore briefly.

Compare this to the love Paul speaks of in the Bible's great "love chapter." Fading? Fickle? A fling? No! Gospel love is tenacious. Like a dog hunkered over a bone, it won't let go. When nothing is left, this love is there to turn out the lights.

Think of that old married couple in the mall, hand in hand, shuffling toward the food court. Better yet, think of Jesus choosing to die for the very ones he knew all along would betray, deny, and desert him. How can you show that same kind of self-sacrificial love to someone in your life?

Your love never fails, it never gives up, never runs out on me.
CHRISTA BLACK GIFFORD, BRIAN JOHNSON,
AND JEREMY RIDDLE

LOVE'S COST

*We know what real love is because Jesus gave
up his life for us. So we also ought to give up
our lives for our brothers and sisters.*

1 JOHN 3:16

To show someone how much you love them, do you go
with the fancy watch or the expensive tools? The dia-
mond earrings or the elegant dinner out?

Whatever gift you settle on, whatever Valentine's
card you choose, remember that real love isn't something
you can buy. You can't order love online and have it gift
wrapped and delivered by UPS.

Real love—God's love—is a sacrifice. It costs us more
than time spent shopping, more than a chunk of our
hard-earned money. Love costs us ourselves. When we go
beyond giving *stuff* to giving our *hearts*, that's when we're
entering the realm of true love.

*To love at all is to be vulnerable. Love anything, and your
heart will certainly be wrung and possibly be broken.*

C. S. LEWIS

WORDS! WORDS! WORDS!

Dear children, let's not merely say that we love each other; let us show the truth by our actions.

1 JOHN 3:18

Eliza Doolittle, the main character in the popular Broadway musical *My Fair Lady*, is courted by a couple of very "wordy" suitors. When she finally gets fed up with all their flowery, romantic expressions, she reprimands them by singing, "Words! Words! Words! I'm so sick of words! . . . Don't talk of stars burning above; if you're in love, show me!"

This is precisely what John is encouraging Christians to do in this frequently quoted verse. It's not enough to talk about our love. We have to show it.

Think of someone in your life. Determine to do one specific loving action today for that person that will speak far louder than any words you could ever say.

Jesus Christ said, "by their fruits ye shall know them," not by their disclaimers.

WILLIAM S. BURROUGHS

WHOLLY HOLY

You must be holy because I, the LORD, am holy. I have set you apart from all other people to be my very own.

LEVITICUS 20:26

Some people think being *holy* means acting "holier than thou." You know, like the Pharisees of the New Testament—being "good" in the worst possible sense of the word. On some lips, the phrase "holy person" means "person to be avoided at all costs."

But consider Jesus. He was holy (i.e., perfect, set apart from evil, and devoted to the Father's purposes). Yet as he moved through the world, the people farthest from God found his life attractive. Sinners flocked to him.

Ask God to help you live for him in holy and beautiful ways today, attracting unholy people to the Good News by your lifestyle.

A Pharisee is hard on others and easy on himself, but a spiritual man is easy on others and hard on himself.

A. W. TOZER

NO MORE LIES

You will know the truth, and the truth will set you free.

JOHN 8:32

Flip this beloved statement of Jesus around and we get something like this: *When we don't know the truth, lies will take us captive.*

That's true, isn't it? Consider just a few of the bogus ideas that imprison so many people:

"I can save myself."

"I'm no good at anything."

"God would never forgive or use me."

"I can either be holy or happy—but not both."

Jesus came to liberate us from such falsehoods with his blunt yet beautiful truth. He began his earthly ministry by declaring that "the oppressed will be set free" (Luke 4:18).

Today, remember his claim: "I am . . . the truth" (John 14:6)—and also that he called the devil "the father of lies" (John 8:44).

The truth will set you free, but first it will make you miserable.

JAMES A. GARFIELD

FEBRUARY 17

NO MATTER WHAT

Even though the fig trees have no blossoms, and there are no grapes on the vines; even though the olive crop fails, and the fields lie empty and barren; even though the flocks die in the fields, and the cattle barns are empty, yet I will rejoice in the LORD! I will be joyful in the God of my salvation!

HABAKKUK 3:17-18

When the prophet Habakkuk complained to God about the moral corruption of his country, God's answer was shocking. He promised to use the Babylonians—an even more wicked nation—to sweep Judah clean!

The prophet spends some time going back and forth questioning God, but by the end of the conversation, Habakkuk's response to the mysterious ways of God is a classic statement of faith and devotion: *No matter how dire the circumstances, I will trust and rejoice in God's sovereignty.*

What surprising ways of God are challenging your faith today?

I gave in, and admitted that God was God.

C. S. LEWIS

MAKING THINGS RIGHT

*God blesses those who hunger and thirst for
justice, for they will be satisfied.*

MATTHEW 5:6

Justice is the pursuit of moral rightness. It works to identify and address wrongs, punish evil, and dismantle oppressive and hurtful systems. It insists that all people be treated fairly.

In confronting religious corruption and in treating women with dignity and children with respect, Jesus embodied justice. His brief ministry gave the world a glimpse of the kind of kingdom he brings—one in which righteousness rules.

It is this hunger and thirst for justice that explains why Christ's followers have always been on the cutting edge of history's great social causes: fighting poverty, slavery, and sex trafficking; advocating for workers; standing up for all who are marginalized.

How can you fight for justice in your world today?

*A man may well be condemned, not for doing
something, but for doing nothing.*

WILLIAM BARCLAY

LISTENING TO GOD

Speak, LORD, your servant is listening.

1 SAMUEL 3:9

Samuel was barely old enough to ride a two-wheeler when God started revealing himself to the boy.

At first Samuel didn't know how to decipher these mysterious nighttime encounters. It was the old priest Eli who taught the boy to pray, "Speak, LORD, your servant is listening."

There's no better prayer for us today—when we open God's Word or when we step out into the world. Like Samuel, each of us was created to play an important role in God's plan.

God *is* speaking. Are you paying attention?

*Every happening, great and small, . . . is a parable whereby
God speaks to us, and the art of life is to get the message.*

MALCOLM MUGGERIDGE

WAVING THE WHITE FLAG

---

*"Abba, Father," [Jesus] cried out, "everything is possible
for you. . . . I want your will to be done, not mine."*

MARK 14:36

We've all been there. You find yourself in a really tough
situation, but not necessarily because you've done anything wrong. It's just one of those tough places in life.
Why? Why would God lead you to such a place? Surely
he wouldn't want this for one of his beloved children,
right?

Jesus shows us how to pray in such moments. He
begins with a right view of God—the Father in heaven
is approachable and all-powerful. And because he cares
about his own, we can honestly pour out our hearts
in times of need. But whatever lies ahead, we can and
should surrender to his plan, knowing his will is always
preferable to our own.

When your will is God's will, you will have your will.
CHARLES H. SPURGEON

SALVATION, NOT JUDGMENT

God sent his Son into the world not to judge the world, but to save the world through him.

JOHN 3:17

Jesus couldn't have been clearer. According to this verse (and many others), he came—at least the first time around—to save, not judge. His message to sinners wasn't an angry denunciation. It was a gracious invitation: "Come to me. Repent. Believe. Follow me, and you'll experience life to the full."

The Bible assures us that Christ will come again. On that occasion, he'll be more Judge than Savior. But for now he waits patiently, giving all people everywhere an opportunity to embrace the Good News.

In light of these truths, join with other Christians in joyfully proclaiming the glorious offer of salvation to the people around you: "Today is the day of salvation" (2 Corinthians 6:2).

You have one business on earth—to save souls.

JOHN WESLEY

WHAT GOD MIGHT DO

Now all glory to God, who is able, through his mighty power at work within us, to accomplish infinitely more than we might ask or think.

EPHESIANS 3:20

It's not hard to see why so many Christians like to read, mull over, and even memorize this verse. It promises that God is able to do not just the great spiritual works we ask him to do but also *more* than we ask—and, in fact, more than we can even dream up!

And the promise gets even better. Notice God's mighty power doesn't merely accomplish more than we can verbalize or fantasize. It produces *infinitely* more.

This means we can approach God in prayer with peace, confidence, and boldness, knowing and expecting that he will answer our requests in unexpected ways.

Expect great things from God; attempt great things for God!

WILLIAM CAREY

PEACE > WORRY

Don't worry about anything; instead, pray about everything.
Tell God what you need, and thank him for all he has
done. Then you will experience God's peace, which
exceeds anything we can understand. His peace will guard
your hearts and minds as you live in Christ Jesus.

PHILIPPIANS 4:6-7

Some people do the opposite: they don't pray about anything; instead, they worry about everything!

Today as you're tempted to fret, turn your anxious thoughts into prayer. Tell God what's got you worked up. Then take time to gratefully recall his past faithfulness.

Experiencing God's peace will not only calm your heart but also protect you from lurking anxious thoughts that want to gain control of you.

If I could hear Christ praying for me in the next
room, I would not fear a million enemies. Yet distance
makes no difference. He is praying for me.
ROBERT MURRAY M'CHEYNE

NEW STRENGTH

Those who trust in the LORD will find new strength.
They will soar high on wings like eagles. They will run
and not grow weary. They will walk and not faint.

ISAIAH 40:31

During the US Civil War, President Abraham Lincoln once muttered, "Sometimes I think I am the tiredest man on earth."

Even if we can't relate to the nightmare of presiding over a nation at war, we all know what it's like to be weary.

Life has a way of draining us dry, but here's God's promise: when our strength is gone, when we feel we can't take even one more step, he is endlessly strong. He will renew us.

Do not strive in your own strength; cast yourself at the
feet of the Lord Jesus, and wait upon Him in the sure
confidence that He is with you and works in you.

ANDREW MURRAY

THE BIBLE IN BRIEF

This is how God loved the world: He gave his
one and only Son, so that everyone who believes
in him will not perish but have eternal life.

JOHN 3:16

Of more than 31,000 verses in the Bible, this is the most popular, most frequently quoted verse of all.

In one sentence we get the story of the universe and the message of the gospel: a God who loves a world of perishing people; a rescue mission involving God's own Son; a promise of endless life to all who believe.

That's the Bible in a nutshell, which begs the questions "Do you believe?" and "Will you share this good news today?"

> *You do not have to know all the theology and all*
> *the right words. You can say, "I am the one He*
> *came to die for." . . . Have that kind of personalized*
> *belief in a personal Lord and Savior.*

A. W. TOZER

SHINE!

Let your good deeds shine out for all to see, so that
everyone will praise your heavenly Father.

MATTHEW 5:16

Here's why "shining for Christ" is tricky: God is the ultimate light (John 1:5), and we were made to reflect his
brightness (Genesis 1:26-28). But sin darkened us and
all creation (Luke 1:78-79). Enter Jesus, the "light of the
world" (John 8:12). He came to call us out of darkness
(1 Peter 2:9). Then he commissioned us to "live as people
of light" (Ephesians 5:8).

Today, if you'll let Christ lead, empower, and shine
through you, you'll radiate a kind of holy glow that
punches holes in the darkness. And you'll call attention
to him.

We are told to let our light shine, and if it does, we won't
need to tell anybody it does. Lighthouses don't fire cannons
to call attention to their shining—they just shine.

D. L. MOODY

WISDOM 101

Cry out for insight, and ask for understanding. Search for them as you would for silver; seek them like hidden treasures. Then you will understand what it means to fear the LORD, and you will gain knowledge of God.

PROVERBS 2:3-5

If it's information you want, there's never been a better time to be alive. Pick a subject, and you can find a web article (if not a whole website) devoted to that topic. Explanatory videos, how-to tutorials—you name it, the Internet's got it.

In Proverbs, Solomon urges us to pursue more than mere information. He argues that wisdom (i.e., skill in living) and the knowledge of God is infinitely more valuable than facts and figures we store in our heads. What good is it, after all, if you know how to retile your bathroom, but you never figure out how to connect with God or get along with others?

As you go about your day, do as Solomon encourages and ask God for wisdom and understanding.

Wisdom . . . consists almost entirely of two parts: the knowledge of God and of ourselves.

JOHN CALVIN

GOOD GOD

*Whatever is good and perfect is a gift coming down to us
from God our Father, who created all the lights in the
heavens. He never changes or casts a shifting shadow.*

JAMES 1:17

Some people see God as cruel, like a kid frying ants with his magnifying glass; or given to unpredictable divine mood swings; or stingy, like a miser hoarding great riches he doesn't even need.

These are all nonbiblical—even demonic—ideas. This popular verse reminds us that God is a loving, unchanging heavenly Father who consistently showers good and perfect gifts upon his children.

Maybe today is a good day to sit down and make a list of the blessings in your life. You might find that you don't have much time for anything else.

*God does not give as we do, a mere trifle to the beggar,
but he bestows his wealth by handsful.*

CHARLES H. SPURGEON

REFLECTING OUR MAKER

*God created human beings in his own image. In the image
of God he created them; male and female he created them.*

GENESIS 1:27

At the most basic level, being made in the image of God
means humans somehow resemble our Maker. Though
we are not divine, we are like God (i.e., we reflect his
nature) in important and unique ways.

We possess intellectual gifts, emotional capacities,
and volitional powers that far transcend those of lesser
creatures. We have exquisite creative ability. We are wired
for relational intimacy. Our souls hunger for love and
justice.

Despite all our glaring flaws and irritating quirks,
humans are still something to behold. Take time today
to praise God for the people he has placed in your life.

*Authentic life is to image God ever more closely by becoming
like Jesus Christ, the express image of the Father.*

NICHOLAS WOLTERSTORFF

RESISTING PRIDE

Humble yourselves before the Lord, and
he will lift you up in honor.

JAMES 4:10

Proud people exalt themselves. They look around and think, *I'm better than these others. I'm more important. My opinions are superior. My agenda is what matters. Everyone—including God—should cater to me.* In short, prideful people play God. They try to control people and events and outcomes.

James rejected such arrogance. Rather than exalting ourselves, he encouraged us to take a humble, childlike posture, admitting that we are sinners in need of God's gracious forgiveness (James 4:7-8).

What great matters do you need to turn over to God today?

The essential vice, the utmost evil, is Pride . . . it was through
Pride that the devil became the devil: Pride leads to every
other vice: it is the complete anti-God state of mind.

C. S. LEWIS

WHAT TIME IS IT?

*For everything there is a season, a time
for every activity under heaven.*

ECCLESIASTES 3:1

Many people quote this famous verse, and the verses that
follow it, in a philosophical, almost resigned way. The
author's almost ambivalent tone can lead the reader to
wonder what faith can offer us in the ups and downs
of life.

It's far better for us to read these words in light of
God's sovereignty. He reigns at all times—when we're
laughing in a maternity ward or weeping in a funeral
home. He's in control when we win and when we lose. All
events and outcomes are in his hands, and, what's more,
the calendar and clock are too.

So whether you're in a season of prosperity or difficulty, it's a good time to remember that our God is
moving your life toward a good end.

*Teach us, O Lord, the disciplines of patience,
for to wait is often harder than to work.*

PETER MARSHALL

THE TEARS OF GOD

Jesus wept.

JOHN 11:35

As one of the shortest verses in the Bible, this popular verse is easy to memorize. However, it's important because it shows the heart of God.

Remember the story? Lazarus, a friend of Jesus, has recently died. His grieving sisters are confused by Jesus' failure to come sooner.

Suddenly Jesus is crying right along with them—despite the fact that he knows he is moments away from resurrecting his friend! Maybe Christ weeps because he sees his friends so brokenhearted. Or perhaps this surge of emotion is because he never meant for his creation to have cemeteries.

Whatever the reason, this much is clear: Jesus reveals a God who weeps with and for us.

Some are men of pleasure, others men of wealth, but He was
"a Man of sorrows." He and sorrow might have changed names.

CHARLES H. SPURGEON

HOLY CONFIDENCE

God has not given us a spirit of fear and timidity,
but of power, love, and self-discipline.

2 TIMOTHY 1:7

Some people aren't just confident; they're convinced that each of their thoughts and all their ideas are brilliant. Oftentimes, these people lock horns with those around them in the furious quest to accomplish their "ingenious" plans. Others are less sure. They constantly second-guess themselves and look over their shoulders. They are afraid to make decisions, lest they choose wrongly.

Noticing that his young protégé tended toward timidity, Paul exhorted Timothy to find a healthy middle ground between the two extremes.

Paul's counsel: God hasn't called us to a lifestyle of reticence. He wants us to live with a balance of strength, concern for others, and healthy self-awareness. Ask God for that kind of confidence today.

When the leader lacks confidence,
the followers lack commitment.

JOHN MAXWELL

DIVINE DELAY

The Lord isn't really being slow about his promise,
as some people think. No, he is being patient
for your sake. He does not want anyone to be
destroyed, but wants everyone to repent.

2 PETER 3:9

The many references in the New Testament to Christ's second coming suggest one thing: the earliest Christians clearly believed the Lord's return was imminent.

Yet here we are almost two thousand years later, still waiting. Why the long delay when there's so much injustice and misery in the world? This verse says it's because there are also so many lost people in the world.

Is the Lord uncaring? No! The truth is because he cares so much about the state and fate of his creation, he waits patiently for more people to turn to him.

When He returns is not as important as the fact that
we are ready for Him when He does return.

A. W. TOZER

MARCH 7

WHAT GOES UP . . .

Pride goes before destruction, and haughtiness
before a fall. Better to live humbly with the poor
than to share plunder with the proud.

PROVERBS 16:18-19

Why does the world rejoice when cocky, oppressive people are humbled? Nobody likes people who put off an arrogant vibe that says, "Look how great I am." We pull for David, not Goliath. We root for Cinderella, not her self-absorbed stepsisters. In short, pride is ugly. True humility is attractive.

This famous proverb says the proud are certain to fall. In the spiritual realm, just as in the physical, whatever goes up—your inflated opinion of yourself, your conceited outlook, your condescending attitude—is destined to come crashing down.

If you have the courage, ask a trusted friend today, "Where do you see signs of pride in my life?" And be ready to make some changes.

They that know God will be humble, and they
that know themselves, cannot be proud.

JOHN FLAVEL

THE KEY TO COURAGE

This is my command—be strong and courageous!
Do not be afraid or discouraged. For the LORD
your God is with you wherever you go.

JOSHUA 1:9

Our English word *courage* comes from a Latin word that means "heart." To have *courage* is to be heartened. To *encourage* others is to put heart or confidence in them. To be *discouraged* is to have a loss of heart.

When Joshua was picked to fill the sandals of the legendary Moses, he—understandably—felt inadequate. So just before the Israelites crossed into the Promised Land, God *encouraged* (or put heart into) Joshua. How? By promising to be with him at all times and in all places.

Let this spiritual truth put heart into you today: the God of the universe is forever with you and in you!

The remedy for discouragement is the Word of God.
WARREN WIERSBE

OVERCOMING ENTROPY

Though our bodies are dying, our spirits are being renewed every day.

2 CORINTHIANS 4:16

Everything about our physical world is breaking down. Entropy is why paint peels, sidewalks crack, and wood rots. In a fallen world, bodies age and ache and die.

But the gospel Paul preached to the people of Corinth says that Jesus breathes new, eternal life into our terminal lives. We may be physically spent and headed toward a hunched-over life in a wheelchair. Spiritually speaking, however, an opposite process is under way. Under the believer's wrinkled skin is a new heart that is being shaped by Jesus. Beneath that gray hair is a mind that is being transformed and renewed.

Take care of your body the best you can. Mostly, take comfort in the truth that Jesus is making all things new.

The God who made us can also remake us.
WOODROW KROLL

GOD'S SPECIAL TREASURE

You are a holy people, who belong to the LORD your God. Of all the people on earth, the LORD your God has chosen you to be his own special treasure.

DEUTERONOMY 7:6

Holy? Chosen? God's *special treasure?* These words of Moses to the Israelites camped on the edge of the Promised Land seem too good to be true.

This ragtag nation was handpicked by God to bless the world, then set apart for his exclusive use. God had a unique affection for them and he valued them infinitely.

In the New Testament, Peter takes these same startling words and applies them to the church of Jesus Christ. That's *us!*

The next time you are feeling insignificant or unsure of your calling, spend a few minutes meditating on this new, true identity.

Our identity rests in God's relentless tenderness for us revealed in Jesus Christ.

BRENNAN MANNING

THE BLESSING IN BEING NEEDY

*God blesses those who are poor and realize their need
for him, for the Kingdom of Heaven is theirs.*

MATTHEW 5:3

Some people seem to have it all—money, connections, health, good looks, talent, social standing. Watching their charmed lives, we fight feelings of envy. *Why are they so blessed?*

Jesus reminds us that things are not what they seem. According to him, the truly blessed aren't the people with everything but those with nothing.

If our lives are continually overflowing with good stuff, where's the need—or time or space—for God? Worldly blessings diminish any sense of needing God; neediness deepens it.

Thank God today for everything in your life that helps you realize your need for him.

*The very thing we dread and are tempted to resist is
actually the means to God's greatest blessings in our lives.*

NANCY LEIGH DEMOSS

COPYING DAD

*Imitate God, therefore, in everything you
do, because you are his dear children.*

EPHESIANS 5:1

Kids go through a cute phase where they mimic their parents. They try on their clothes and become little shadows. When Dad begins cutting the grass, Junior grabs his toy mower and makes a beeline for the front lawn.

In this verse we see the command to imitate our Father in heaven. Does this mean we strain to be godly? No, that kind of imitation leads only to spiritual frustration. True godliness requires letting Christ live his perfect, powerful life in and through us (Galatians 2:20).

It's by trusting Jesus that we love, give, and forgive like God. Such a life is more than a cute phase; it's a beautiful existence.

*Godliness is not the consequence of your capacity
to imitate God but the consequence of His
capacity to reproduce Himself in you.*

W. IAN THOMAS

PUTTING OTHERS FIRST

Don't be selfish; don't try to impress others. Be humble,
thinking of others as better than yourselves. Don't look out
only for your own interests, but take an interest in others, too.

PHILIPPIANS 2:3-4

Western culture is unabashedly about "self." We applaud those who are self-made (i.e., self-starters who self-promote and end up being self-sufficient). We're encouraged to have self-esteem, to engage in self-help, to be self-indulgent, and to take lots of selfies. No wonder we're so self-conscious, self-centered, and self-absorbed!

This passage says no to all that selfish thinking and living. Put others first, Paul says. Consider what they need. Take into account their interests. And if you aren't sure what that looks like, look at Christ.

What's one practical way you can put others first today?

Above all the grace and the gifts that Christ gives
to his beloved is that of overcoming self.

FRANCIS OF ASSISI

MARCH 14

PRAY FOR OUR LEADERS

I urge you, first of all, to pray for all people. Ask God to help them; intercede on their behalf, and give thanks for them. Pray this way for kings and all who are in authority.

1 TIMOTHY 2:1-2

It's the appropriate answer to every government-related complaint: pray for our leaders. And what a blessed privilege that is! To be able to bring men and women by name before the God who created them and say, "Please, Father, help them to use their positions of authority to bring you glory."

Pray today for your local and national leaders that the Lord would help them in their work.

May that Being who is supreme over all, the Patron of Order, the Fountain of Justice, and the Protector in all ages of the world of virtuous liberty, continue His blessing upon this nation and its Government and give it all possible success and duration consistent with the ends of His providence.

JOHN ADAMS

THE RULES OF LOVE

You have heard the law that says, "Love your neighbor" and hate your enemy. But I say, love your enemies! Pray for those who persecute you!

MATTHEW 5:43-44

Most people have two basic rules of love concerning other people: (1) love your family and friends, and (2) love your neighbors. Neither of these two rules are particularly noteworthy. Loving those who love us and treating others well just so they'll return the favor seem more like self-love.

Jesus added a third rule: (3) love your enemies. Go out of your way to bless those people who hate you and make your life miserable. And pray for them too. Jesus showed he wasn't speaking hypothetically when he prayed from the cross, "Father, forgive them, for they don't know what they are doing" (Luke 23:34).

What enemy do you need to love for Christ's sake?

The Bible tells us to love our neighbors, and also to love our enemies; probably because they are generally the same people.

G. K. CHESTERTON

ULTIMATE LOVE

*He gave up his divine privileges; he took the humble
position of a slave and was born as a human being.
When he appeared in human form, he humbled himself
in obedience to God and died a criminal's death on a cross.*

PHILIPPIANS 2:7-8

Sometimes it's not easy to feel loved. The world works to convince us that we are *not* loved, but the Cross says otherwise. Even if you were the only person on earth, the only person to ever sin, Jesus still would have died for you because he loves you—with an ultimate, incomprehensible love.

When you're having trouble feeling this love, revisit the Gospel accounts of Jesus' gift to you.

*We sinned for no reason but an incomprehensible
lack of love, and He saved us for no reason
but an incomprehensible excess of love.*

PETER KREEFT

THE SECRET OF LIFE

*Trust in the LORD with all your heart; do not depend
on your own understanding. Seek his will in all you
do, and he will show you which path to take.*

PROVERBS 3:5-6

Why are so many people enamored with this passage?
Because this is the secret of life, the road map, if you will.
Don't trust in yourself; don't rely on your own ideas of
what *seems* wise. (Adam and Eve tried that—look where
it got them.)

On the contrary, trust the Lord with everything
you've got. Listen eagerly to his Word; then faithfully
do it. If you seek him and his will, he will show you the
way to go.

Though it sounds so simple, it's not always easy. We'll
spend the rest of our lives trying to get it right.

*[People] think faith is a big electric blanket,
when of course it is the cross.*
FLANNERY O'CONNOR

A WAY OUT

*The temptations in your life are no different from what
others experience. And God is faithful. He will not allow the
temptation to be more than you can stand. When you are
tempted, he will show you a way out so that you can endure.*

1 CORINTHIANS 10:13

Some sinful impulses feel irresistible, don't they? But
what if God has made a way for us to escape temptation's
lure—every single time?

This much-quoted verse gives a magnificent promise:
our faithful God will never let us face irresistible temptation, and he will always show us a way out. That out
may be as simple as running from a room. It might be as
radical as quitting your job.

In the temptation you're facing, what way out do
you see?

*Temptations are like stray cats—treat one nice, and
before you know it, it'll be back with all of its friends!*

UNKNOWN

FAITH AND ACTION

*What good is it, dear brothers and sisters, if you say
you have faith but don't show it by your actions?
Can that kind of faith save anyone?*

JAMES 2:14

Faith for some is a noun. It's all the theological ideas to which one subscribes. In this view, if you say, "I believe Jesus is the Son of God who died on the cross for my sins," you're regarded as "saved."

Other Christians insist that saving faith is more verb than noun. It might begin with acknowledging certain biblical ideas, but it always culminates in action.

Genuine faith is both—our verb ("response") to God's noun ("revelation"). A saving faith is accompanied by actions that flow from a heart filled with love and gratitude.

*While the mind is occupied in inquiring,
"Do I believe or feel this thing right?" the true question
is forgotten: "Have I left all to follow him?"*
GEORGE MACDONALD

SPIRIT-TAUGHT

*That is what the Scriptures mean when they say,
"No eye has seen, no ear has heard, and no mind has
imagined what God has prepared for those who love him."*

1 CORINTHIANS 2:9

At first glance, it seems this verse describes how amazing heaven will be. But it's really about our ability to understand spiritual truths—now *and* in the future.

Here Paul is contrasting worldly wisdom with God's wisdom. The Lord gives spiritual insight not to those who are clever or smart but to those who humbly love him. Paul quotes from Isaiah 64:4 to make the point that we can't acquire spiritual understanding via human ingenuity (i.e., eyes, ears, thoughts). Rather, it is revealed by the Spirit of God himself.

Reason alone cannot lead us to God. We must be Spirit-taught.

*The most brilliant intellect may be imbecilic
when confronted with the mysteries of God.*

A. W. TOZER

STANDING INVITATION

---

*Let us come boldly to the throne of our gracious
God. There we will receive his mercy, and we will
find grace to help us when we need it most.*

HEBREWS 4:16

People with problems can't just barge into the Oval
Office. An appointment with the president requires
powerful connections. Even if you pass the background
checks, you have to be scheduled far in advance. If you're
lucky, you might get five whole minutes to meet with the
leader of the nation.

It's not like this for the children of God. We can come
boldly (i.e., confidently, not irreverently) into God's presence anytime—no appointment needed. When we need
mercy and grace the most, we can be sure he will give it.

What problem do you need to bring to God today?
What's your hesitation?

*Prayer means that we have come boldly into the throne
room and we are standing in God's presence.*

E. W. KENYON

THE ULTIMATE CONNECTION

I am the vine; you are the branches. Those who remain in me, and I in them, will produce much fruit. For apart from me you can do nothing.

JOHN 15:5

Connection is the new buzzword. Businesses want to *connect* to their customers. Churches want their members to *connect* with one another. In this classic passage, Jesus speaks of the reality of spiritual connection.

The Bible says that at salvation we were joined to Christ. From then on, the whole of our Christian experience is learning how to live in this reality. "Remain in me" is how Jesus put it. In other words, "Stay attached to me. Draw your life from me."

Just as a branch withers when it's separated from the vine, so we wilt when we disconnect from Christ. Stay connected today!

We must look away from our own person. Christ and my conscience must become one, so that I can see nothing else but Christ crucified and raised from the dead for me. If I keep looking at myself, I am gone.

MARTIN LUTHER

BLANK CHECK?

*If you remain in me and my words remain in you, you
may ask for anything you want, and it will be granted!*

JOHN 15:7

"Ask for anything you want," Jesus said. It's an eyebrow-raising statement—a seeming "blank check" from God. Does this mean as Christ's followers we can start requesting expensive cars and luxury vacations?

Read the verse again. Note the conditions: "if you remain in me and my words remain in you." In other words, *Stick close to me and let my truth permeate and shape your life. When that happens, my values, desires, and purposes will become yours. That's when you'll pray the kinds of prayers that I pray. And such prayers are the kind our Father in heaven is sure to answer.*

*Our prayers run along one road and God's answers
by another, and by and by they meet.*

ADONIRAM JUDSON

DOLING OUT GRACE

God has given each of you a gift from his great variety
of spiritual gifts. Use them well to serve one another.

1 PETER 4:10

In ancient times, the most trustworthy servants were called *stewards*. Their job description was simple: carry out the master's will by using the master's resources to help family members or fellow servants.

Similarly, Christians are servants of Christ who have been entrusted with spiritual abilities and material blessings. We are to steward (i.e., manage) all of God's gifts in the service of others.

When we withhold our gifts, others miss out. And if we refuse to use the resources the Master has given us to bless others, it will no doubt lead to an uncomfortable conversation one day (2 Corinthians 5:10).

If my life is fruitless, it doesn't matter who praises me,
and if my life is fruitful, it doesn't matter who criticizes me.

JOHN BUNYAN

KEPT FROM FALLING

*Now all glory to God, who is able to keep you from
falling away and will bring you with great joy into
his glorious presence without a single fault.*

JUDE 1:24

In the early church, certain influential teachers propagated false ideas about God. As a result, many fell away from the true faith. Jude wrote to believers to encourage them to stand firm and fix their hopes on the gospel. This great benediction is a hymn of praise to the God who pledges to see his children all the way home.

Two thousand years after Jude wrote these words, impostors still fill pulpits, bookstores, and the Internet with bad theology. Be careful and trust God. The more you know his Word, the less likely you are to be tricked by purveyors of error.

*This would be the first step in apostasy; men first
forget the true, and then adore the false.*

CHARLES H. SPURGEON

PASS IT ON

*You have heard me teach things that have been confirmed
by many reliable witnesses. Now teach these truths to other
trustworthy people who will be able to pass them on to others.*

2 TIMOTHY 2:2

Every Christian needs a Paul and a Timothy.

A "Paul" is a mentor—someone who's been around the spiritual block a few more times than you. When you spend time with a Paul, you find encouragement. A "Timothy" is a younger person with whom you share principles, lessons, and skills you've picked up along the way.

See the model? Paul → Timothy → others.

Programs have their place, but the biggest impact happens when one person pours into another. Who's *your* Paul? Who's *your* Timothy?

*We are constantly on a stretch, if not on a strain, to
devise new methods, new plans, new organizations to
advance . . . the gospel. . . . Men are God's method.*

EDWARD M. BOUNDS

JESUS UNDERSTANDS

This High Priest of ours understands our weaknesses, for he faced all of the same testings we do, yet he did not sin.

HEBREWS 4:15

On the nightly news, you watch someone pick through the rubble of his tornado-ravaged home. You think, *I can't imagine!* Your heart goes out—and your prayers go up. This is *sympathy.*

Another person watches and vividly remembers her personal experience of having to pick up the pieces. Since she survived a tornado, she understands. This is *empathy.*

This verse reminds us that because Jesus has faced temptations and trials, he's been where we are. He knows what you face. Today, when sin comes knocking, turn to the sympathetic *and* empathetic one. He understands. And he can give you victory.

Christ, because He was the only man who never yielded to temptation, is also the only man who knows to the full what temptation means.

C. S. LEWIS

HOUSE ON A ROCK

*Anyone who listens to my teaching and follows it is
wise, like a person who builds a house on solid rock.*

MATTHEW 7:24

Jesus makes no bones about it: a house built on the
world's way of life will fall, but a house built on his Word
will stand strong. But we must do more than just *listen*
to his Word—we must *obey* it (see James 1:22). We must
take it into our hearts, agree with it, surrender to it, and
do what it says. Then we get to enjoy the peace and stability of a life lived under the shelter of God's arms.

As you study the words of Jesus, ask him which teachings he would have you focus on obeying today.

*It does not require great learning to be a Christian and
to be convinced of the truth of the Bible. It requires
only an honest heart and a willingness to obey God.*

WILLIAM BARNES

CHARIOTS OF FIRE

Don't be afraid! . . . For there are more
on our side than on theirs!

2 KINGS 6:16

What do the Bible and fantasy/sci-fi movies have in common? At least one thing: a steadfast conviction that there's more to reality than meets the eye.

In 2 Kings 6, when Elisha and his servant find themselves surrounded by enemy troops, they don't get transported to a parallel universe. Nor do they find a secret portal or passageway to an unknown realm like Narnia or Middle-earth. However, God does give them a brief, stunning glimpse of invisible spiritual realities. All about them, they see "horses and chariots of fire" (6:17)—God's protection.

If God likewise pulled back the curtains to show you the spiritual reality today, it's safe to say you wouldn't have even one moment of fear. Pray for eyes to see.

Faith sees the invisible, believes the unbelievable,
and receives the impossible.

CORRIE TEN BOOM

KNOWING WHERE
WE STAND

Jesus Christ is the same yesterday, today, and forever.

HEBREWS 13:8

Immutability is the quality of being unchangeable. When used of the Lord, it means that he possesses an eternal sameness. He is rock steady and consistent. His character doesn't vary. He doesn't alter, amend, or adjust his will.

This is comforting for thousands of reasons. It means we don't have to worry about divine mood swings. It means God's promises don't have expiration dates. It means his plans don't vacillate from day to day.

In a world where nothing remains as is—where people leave and health fades and jobs go away and possessions wear out—we have an unchanging anchor. Today, take some time to praise the one who can be counted on no matter what.

Consider what you owe to His immutability. Though you have changed a thousand times, He has not changed once.

CHARLES H. SPURGEON

MARCH 31

FILLED

*Everyone present was filled with the Holy
Spirit and began speaking in other languages,
as the Holy Spirit gave them this ability.*

ACTS 2:4

The birth of the church was a deluge of wind and fire.
This was followed by believers declaring the message of
Jesus in languages they had not previously known.

Some see this moment as *prescriptive*—dictating the
experience that all believers in every era should have.
Others see it as *descriptive*—such miracles happened to
them, but who knows what will happen when the Spirit
of God Almighty moves in us?

God is in charge of bestowing gifts and determining
outcomes. Our responsibility is to be yielded to the Spirit
and wholly available for his use.

*The Spirit-filled life is not a special, deluxe
edition of Christianity. It is part and parcel
of the total plan of God for His people.*

A. W. TOZER

THE INVITATION

Jesus said, "Come to me, all of you who are weary and carry heavy burdens, and I will give you rest."

MATTHEW 11:28

Secular Greek writers sometimes used this word *weary* to refer to a beating. In other words, Jesus wasn't talking here to people who needed a nap. He was addressing people who were beaten down by a life and a culture that had left them worn out and feeling hopeless. What's worse, in that depleted state, they carried the weight of the world.

Maybe that's you today. You're spiritually spent. You can't keep going. And you're lugging around a big tiresome load of guilt, shame, pressure, and regret.

Jesus says, "Come . . . I will give you rest." Will you believe him?

You have made us for yourself, and our heart is restless until it rests in you.

AUGUSTINE OF HIPPO

APRIL 2

THE YOKE OF JESUS

Take my yoke upon you. Let me teach you,
because I am humble and gentle at heart,
and you will find rest for your souls.

MATTHEW 11:29

Jesus promises rest to the spiritually exhausted. But rather than prescribing a week at the beach, he talks about yokes. In case you didn't grow up in the country, a yoke is a farm implement that fits over the heads of two animals so they can pull a wagon or plow together. In other words, yokes are for work, not R & R.

Jesus is saying here, "Come alongside me. Link up with me. I'll show you a better way, and I'll even do all the heavy lifting."

Religion without grace typically involves pride and harshness—and no rest. Doesn't the humble, gentle, restful way of Jesus sound better?

When sin is your burden, Christ will be your delight.
THOMAS WATSON

A BEARABLE LOAD

My yoke is easy to bear, and the burden I give you is light.

MATTHEW 11:30

Religion says we have to work our way into God's good graces. The gospel says, no, we are made right with God because of what Jesus did.

But if we aren't saved *by* good works, we are saved *for* good works (Ephesians 2:8-10). Jesus invites us to join him in what he's doing in the world. "Partner with me," he essentially says. "I'll give you tasks that match your abilities and gifts."

If the yoke you're wearing is wearing you out, it's not Jesus' yoke. His promise is that when we link our lives to him, go where he leads, and do what he gives us to do, we find fulfillment, not exhaustion. We experience blessing, not burden.

A burden shared is a lighter load.
WOODROW KROLL

CALM UNDER FIRE

The LORD himself will fight for you. Just stay calm.

EXODUS 14:14

Remember this scene? The Israelites are trapped between the Red Sea and the fearsome Egyptian army, which is thundering toward them. They're common laborers, not trained warriors! Even if they had weapons, they wouldn't know how to use them! As the people of God begin to panic, Moses speaks these comforting and beloved words.

God would later command his people to engage in battle (Joshua 8:1; Ephesians 6:12; 1 Timothy 6:12). But on this day he called his people to stand still and let him fight on their behalf.

Whatever battles you're facing, ask God, "What is my role here?" Do that, and leave the rest—especially the results—to him.

There's nothing more calming in difficult moments than knowing there's someone fighting with you.

MOTHER TERESA

ULTIMATE DEPENDABILITY

God is not a man, so he does not lie. He is not human, so he does not change his mind. Has he ever spoken and failed to act? Has he ever promised and not carried it through?

NUMBERS 23:19

Some people smile at you even as they lie to you. Others make commitments that last only until they decide they're sick of being committed! Whom can you depend on?

In this famous passage, the prophet Balaam tells King Balak of Moab he can't call down curses on Israel, because God has promised to bless Israel! If God were human, he could be bought off or pressured to change his mind. But God isn't like us. We might be fickle, but he is faithful.

What trustworthy promise of God are you clinging to today?

*Great is thy faithfulness, O God, my Father,
there is no shadow of turning with thee.*

THOMAS CHISHOLM

DANGEROUS INVESTMENTS

Don't store up treasures here on earth, where moths eat them and rust destroys them, and where thieves break in and steal.

MATTHEW 6:19

Is it wiser to invest in real estate or commodities? Technology stocks or tax-free bonds? Cattle futures or cash? How about silver and gold? Fine art? Ask ten certified financial planners and you'll get ten different responses.

Ask Jesus, and he'll tell you that no earthly investment is safe. Fraud is an ever-present reality, and global events can, at any moment, trigger a market collapse, making even the most diversified portfolio extremely vulnerable.

Is your security and hope in earthly treasures? If so, what would you do if those assets were suddenly gone?

Money never stays with me. It would burn me if it did. I throw it out of my hands as soon as possible, lest it should find its way into my heart.

JOHN WESLEY

A VERSE ABOUT PARENTING

Direct your children onto the right path, and when they are older, they will not leave it.

PROVERBS 22:6

This proverb, so cherished by Christian parents, sounds like a formula for successful child-rearing: teach your kids about Jesus, keep them in church, send them to camp, and have family devotions—and they will love God passionately all their days.

Try telling this to faithful parents who have grown prodigal children.

When reading wisdom literature, it's important to understand that proverbs are general observations about how life works, not surefire guarantees. They're principles, not promises. Consider this: if God gave us formulas, why would we ever need faith?

If you're a parent, keep faithfully pointing your kids toward Christ (and keep praying like crazy)!

Let no Christian parents fall into the delusion that the Sunday school is intended to ease them of their personal duties.

CHARLES H. SPURGEON

WORTHWHILE WORK

Unless the LORD builds a house, the work of the builders is wasted. Unless the LORD protects a city, guarding it with sentries will do no good.

PSALM 127:1

Think of all the projects that are launched independent of God. In many marriages, businesses, college careers, and philanthropic endeavors, God is not even a passing thought. His glory isn't pursued. The new venture is about bringing pleasure (or money and fame) to an individual or group. His wisdom isn't sought; only human "experts" are consulted. His power isn't relied upon; all work is done in human strength.

This passage speaks to the vanity (and perhaps insanity?) of doing anything apart from God. Ask yourself: "Is God the catalyst, provider, and sustainer of all that I'm doing today?"

I used to ask God to help me. Then I asked if I might help Him. I ended up by asking Him to do His work through me.

HUDSON TAYLOR

GOOD GRIEF!

God blesses those who mourn, for they will be comforted.

MATTHEW 5:4

The blessing Jesus speaks about in this verse (and the "beatitudes" that precede and follow it) means a happy thing, a fortunate turn of events. Jesus is saying that suffering and loss can lead to blessing. Does that seem crazy to you? It's not.

Those who mourn are assured the comfort of God (see also 2 Corinthians 1:3-4). He doesn't promise to take away our sorrows, only to be with us in our grief. Mourning also keeps us dependent. Life's fragility and unpredictability remind us continually of our immense need for God.

For the believer, then, grief can actually be good—not fun, but profitable. There is blessing in brokenness.

I thought I could . . . make a map of sorrow. Sorrow,
however, turns out to be not a state but a process.

C. S. LEWIS

THE GREAT PROMISE

*I tell you the truth, those who listen to my message
and believe in God who sent me have eternal life.
They will never be condemned for their sins,
but they have already passed from death into life.*

JOHN 5:24

This verse is for everyone who wonders where they stand
with God. It's for those who are uncertain about their
eternal destination.

"Listen," Jesus said. That is, "Perk up. Pay attention.
Take my words to heart." "Believe," Jesus said. In other
words, "Trust that I am who I say I am—a Savior sent
from God."

Those who do these things "have eternal life" and
"will never be condemned." By faith, they have "passed
from death into life." Whom can you share this great
promise with today?

*Christianity is a statement which, if false, is of no
importance, and, if true, of infinite importance.
The one thing it cannot be is moderately important.*

C. S. LEWIS

APRIL 11

UNDER THE INFLUENCE

Don't be drunk with wine, because that will ruin
your life. Instead, be filled with the Holy Spirit.

EPHESIANS 5:18

"Under the influence" is an apt description for drunkenness. When people overindulge, they don't just *drive* erratically, they *speak* thoughtlessly and *act* with almost no inhibitions.

The apostle Paul used intoxication to illustrate the filling of the Spirit. Similar to the way alcohol takes over a person and alters one's behavior, the Spirit of God becomes a controlling influence in the life of a Christian who surrenders to him.

Though the Spirit resides in every believer, not every believer operates under his influence all the time. Ask God to put you under the influence of his Spirit.

A holy life is impossible apart from the enabling of the Holy Spirit.

It may be said without qualification that every man is
as holy and as full of the Spirit as he wants to be.

A. W. TOZER

WHEN IT ALL
FADES AWAY

*Heaven and earth will disappear,
but my words will never disappear.*

MARK 13:31

Shortly before his death, sitting on the Mount of Olives, Jesus reminded his disciples of the temporal nature of earth by telling them that heaven and earth will be destroyed. In fact, cataclysmic judgment is coming (2 Peter 3:7, 10-13). After that, the whole universe will undergo a breathtaking re-creation (Revelation 21:1).

But in this fading world, where nothing is permanent, Jesus assures his followers that his words are eternal—they will never be destroyed.

Take heart. God's truth will forever be true. His promises won't ever expire. We have enduring hope so long as we cling to Christ's teachings.

What can you do specifically today to root the eternal words of Jesus in your heart?

*The permanence of God's character guarantees
the fulfillment of His promises.*

A. W. PINK

APRIL 13

DIVINE ACCESS

*Jesus uttered another loud cry and breathed his
last. And the curtain in the sanctuary of the
Temple was torn in two, from top to bottom.*

MARK 15:37-38

Several amazing miracles occurred at the time of Christ's
crucifixion: a solar eclipse (Luke 23:45); tombs opening after an earthquake and bodies being raised from the
dead (Matthew 27:51-53); and the tearing of the Temple
curtain.

Once a year, Israel's high priest would disappear
behind this thick curtain into the Temple's Most Holy
Place and offer a sacrifice for the sins of the people.

This miraculous ripping of the veil shows that by his
sacrificial death, Jesus opened a permanent way of access
to God. The fact that the tear was from top to bottom
is enough to give any thoughtful person goose bumps.

*The Christian is a holy rebel loose in the
world with access to the throne of God.*

A. W. TOZER

RISEN FROM THE DEAD

The angel said, "Don't be alarmed. You are looking
for Jesus of Nazareth, who was crucified. He isn't here!
He is risen from the dead! Look, this is where they laid
his body. Now go and tell his disciples, including Peter,
that Jesus is going ahead of you to Galilee. You will
see him there, just as he told you before he died."

MARK 16:6-7

On Friday Jesus' disciples were so scared, they scattered. Saturday found them depressed and all but destroyed.

Then came the wild events of Sunday: the angel's announcement, the tomb with no body, assorted appearances by a very-much-alive Jesus.

"He is risen from the dead! . . . You will see him." What else can explain the disciples' remarkable transformation from flaky to fearless?

You can also live in the fearlessness of Jesus' resurrection. Will you invite the resurrected Christ to live in and through you today?

Perhaps the transformation of the disciples of Jesus is
the greatest evidence of all for the resurrection.

JOHN STOTT

TRUE RELIGION

No, O people, the LORD has told you what is good,
and this is what he requires of you: to do what is right,
to love mercy, and to walk humbly with your God.

MICAH 6:8

Legalism is sneaky. If we're not careful, our quest for perfection can trick us into thinking that the only way to please God is to stay extra busy doing "churchy" things.

The prophet Micah warned the ancient people of God against a preoccupation with external behaviors. Instead of trying to please God by completing some kind of daily religious to-do list, Micah urged an inside-out approach: humility before God along with a heart that yearns for righteousness and for God's mercy to be extended to others.

True religion is cultivating a godly heart first and *then* reaping the rewards of a godly life.

The heart of every problem is the problem in the heart.
WARREN WIERSBE

THE WAY TO PRAY

*Pray like this: Our Father in heaven, may your name
be kept holy. May your Kingdom come soon. May
your will be done on earth, as it is in heaven.*

MATTHEW 6:9-10

It's easy for our prayers to become all about us, isn't it?
After all, we feel like we have major needs. Who better
to help than God?

So how do we avoid sounding so self-absorbed, as if
we're giving our wish lists to Santa?

Jesus teaches us to pray first that the Father's name
would be honored, that his rule as King would come
imminently, and that his will (not ours) would come to
pass.

When we begin our prayers with this kind of God-
centered focus, we can focus appropriately on God and
others, rather than ourselves only.

*Our prayers should arise out of immersion in the
Scripture. . . . This wedding of the Bible and
prayer anchors your life down in the real God.*

TIM KELLER

NO LIMITS!

His unfailing love toward those who fear him is as great as
the height of the heavens above the earth. He has removed
our sins as far from us as the east is from the west.

PSALM 103:11-12

Some believers sadly embrace a scarcity mind-set. They put false limits on God's infinite resources. For example, they might outwardly claim, "God loves me!" while inwardly thinking, *So long as I don't do anything really terrible.* Or they might say, "God has completely forgiven me!" while thinking, *Unless I make a regular habit of messing up.*

According to this beloved psalm, the blessings of God are infinite. His love is bigger than the universe. His promise to remove our sins is unconditional; it's full and final.

Do you believe that? Or do you put limits on God's love and forgiveness?

> *You [God] are good and all-powerful, caring for each*
> *one of us as though the only one in your care.*
> AUGUSTINE OF HIPPO

APRIL 18

MOTIVE MATTERS

*Whether you eat or drink, or whatever you
do, do it all for the glory of God.*

1 CORINTHIANS 10:31

In each human heart, and in every human interaction,
a hodgepodge of motives battles for supremacy. Pride is
always lurking. Greed, fear, envy, and lust are seeking
to rear their ugly heads. Sometimes it is pain or anger
that wins the day. In our best moments, we are powered
by love.

Here Paul champions the motive of *determining to
glorify God*. In every situation, in whatever you do, seek
to honor God.

How can you make much of God today in whatever
you might be doing—driving, exercising, surfing online,
working, cooking, parenting, shopping, snacking? How
about while doing chores or having a conversation?

Whatever you do, let your motive be the glory of God.

A Christian should be an Alleluia from head to foot.
AUGUSTINE OF HIPPO

THE GREAT ANTIDOTE

Humble yourselves before God.
Resist the devil, and he will flee from you.

JAMES 4:7

In his modern classic *Mere Christianity*, C. S. Lewis called pride "The Great Sin." He argued convincingly that pride is behind all the misery in the world, and he wryly observed that it was through self-exalting pride that the devil became the devil!

No wonder the book of James commands us to humble ourselves. Proud people wreak havoc in living rooms, bedrooms, boardrooms, and classrooms. But the humble are God-centered and others-focused—the very opposite of self-absorbed and self-promoting. In their holy fear of God, and with a healthy perspective on the devil, the humble sow seeds of peace, not discord.

In what situation today do you need to beware of pride?

A really humble man . . . will not be thinking about
humility: he will not be thinking about himself at all.

C. S. LEWIS

ACCEPTABLE BOASTING

This is what the LORD says: "Don't let the wise boast in their wisdom, or the powerful boast in their power, or the rich boast in their riches. But those who wish to boast should boast in this alone: that they truly know me and understand that I am the LORD who demonstrates unfailing love and who brings justice and righteousness to the earth, and that I delight in these things. I, the LORD, have spoken!"

JEREMIAH 9:23-24

People boast about lots of things: being smart or good-looking, wealthy or athletic, successful or powerful.

Jeremiah reminds us that the only thing worth bragging about is a relationship with God. Everything else is futile and fleeting. God's love is the only thing that lasts.

And lest we get overconfident, let us remember that we know God *only because of his grace.*

Grace puts its hand on their boasting mouth, and shuts it once for all.

CHARLES SPURGEON

APRIL 21

TALK IS CHEAP

*The Kingdom of God is not just a lot of
talk; it is living by God's power.*

1 CORINTHIANS 4:20

Ancient Corinth was filled with spiritually minded
people spouting all kinds of thoughts about God. Paul
responded, "Talk is cheap. Give me a life marked by
God's power any day."

If ever there were a verse for this generation, this is it.
Think of how easy it is to post "Christian viewpoints,"
Bible verses, and deep spiritual thoughts on social media.

Such things aren't bad for the most part—unless we
drift into angry ranting. It's just that actions, as the old
saying goes, speak much louder than words.

Remember: to save the world, God didn't send a text
or even a sermon. He sent a Savior.

Let there be something of benevolence, in all that I speak.
JONATHAN EDWARDS

CLEAN!

*If we confess our sins to him, he is faithful and just to
forgive us our sins and to cleanse us from all wickedness.*

1 JOHN 1:9

A Christian sins. That person knew the right course of
action but chose to defy God—for one or more foolish
reasons. What then?

This verse urges us as believers to confess our sins.
The Greek word John used here means "to say the same
thing." That's confession—saying the same things about
our sins that God says about them. We agree with God
that our sins are offensive, that Christ paid for them at
the Cross, and that we don't have to yield to them in the
future.

And the glorious promise to those who do this from
a sincere heart: full forgiveness and cleansing from our
faithful and righteous God.

After grief for sin there should be joy for forgiveness.

A. W. PINK

SUFFERING SERVANT

He was pierced for our rebellion, crushed for
our sins. He was beaten so we could be whole.
He was whipped so we could be healed.

ISAIAH 53:5

In Jesus' day, the Jews were expecting a triumphant Messiah-King, a mighty warrior like David, who would rout Israel's enemies and restore the nation to its former glory. They didn't realize that the Scripture foretold of a suffering servant-Messiah.

Jesus endured unimaginable suffering "for our rebellion . . . for our sins . . . so we could be whole . . . so we could be healed."

Before the Messiah rules the whole earth, he intends to repair and reign over our rebellious hearts. Today, let the one who died for you live in you.

We are more sinful and flawed in ourselves than we
ever dared believe, yet . . . we are more loved and
accepted in Jesus Christ than we ever dared hope.

TIMOTHY KELLER

APRIL 24

CRY MERCY!

In your great mercy, you did not destroy
them completely or abandon them forever.
What a gracious and merciful God you are!

NEHEMIAH 9:31

For no reason, the little brother whacks the big brother.
The big brother wrestles his smaller sibling to the ground,
sits on his chest, and says, "Cry mercy"—in other words,
"You've wronged me, but if you'll just admit it, I'll let
you go."

It's an imperfect analogy, just a dim picture of God's
astonishing mercy. Instead of justice, the guilty are met
with kindness. They escape the grim consequences their
sins deserve.

In the book of Nehemiah we read that the ancient
Israelites spent a day in worship and confession, praising
God for responding repeatedly to their stubborn sinful-
ness with stunning mercy. We should do likewise.

God's mercy with a sinner is only equaled and perhaps
outmatched by His patience with the saints, with you and me.

ALAN REDPATH

SECURITY AND STABILITY

God is my strong fortress, and he makes my way
perfect. He makes me as surefooted as a deer,
enabling me to stand on mountain heights.

2 SAMUEL 22:33-34

Sometimes the world feels dangerous and our own lives feel precarious. What then?

Here King David gives thanks to God for his protection and provision. Specifically, he expresses gratitude for the way God has hidden him from danger ("my strong fortress") and the way God has helped him through danger ("makes me as surefooted as a deer, enabling me to stand").

The image of a deer nimbly making its way across a steep mountainside is comforting to anyone who feels shaky. If you're facing an uphill climb over and around big obstacles, God can keep you from tumbling. Whatever lies ahead, trust him to save, steady, and strengthen you.

I arise today, through God's strength to pilot me.

ST. PATRICK

APRIL 26

THE BIG PICTURE

He has planted eternity in the human heart,
but even so, people cannot see the whole scope
of God's work from beginning to end.

ECCLESIASTES 3:11

Have you ever gotten a good seat at a parade? A comfy spot where you can watch all the fun floats and talented people pass by? This view of the parade brings you much joy, but you can't see where the parade starts or where it ends from this spot, can you?

God can see it all. He sees the beginning and the end and every viewpoint in between. We can't—so we must trust God to perfectly orchestrate the parade, and just enjoy the view he's gifted us.

The will of God is never exactly what you expect
it to be. It may seem to be much worse, but in the
end it's going to be a lot better and a lot bigger.

ELISABETH ELLIOT

LIFE'S TOUGH STUFF

Dear brothers and sisters, when troubles of any kind come your way, consider it an opportunity for great joy.

JAMES 1:2

When troubles come, do you inwardly freak and outwardly fret? Do you complain? Cry? Curse? Give God the cold shoulder, then give in to despair?

The apostle James urges a radically different response. Rejoice, he says. Here's why: trials grow us and make us wise. Hanging on during hard times strengthens our faith and shapes our hearts (much like sticking with a grueling workout regimen shapes our bodies). Tests will—if we let them—push us toward the Lord.

Let's be clear: we don't experience much *happiness* in the midst of life's storms, but we can find *joy*. God promises to be with us during our troubles and to transform us through them.

Faithless is he that says farewell when the road darkens.
GIMLI IN *THE FELLOWSHIP OF THE RING*
BY J. R. R. TOLKIEN

ALL OUT IN LOVE

*Most important of all, continue to show deep love for
each other, for love covers a multitude of sins.*

1 PETER 4:8

You've probably seen pictures of Olympic sprinters straining with all their might to cross the finish line. That's the word picture Peter paints for how followers of Jesus are to love one another: with total focus and all-out effort.

In short, Christian love isn't weak or wishy-washy. It's strong enough to meet any challenge.

Peter says this kind of powerful love covers (i.e., hides) the failures of others. This is different from the old expression "love is blind." Romantic love may be starry-eyed; Christian love is clear-eyed. Like Jesus, we see people, warts and all. But gospel love chooses to overlook and forgive—even when the other isn't exactly lovable.

*The world does not understand theology or dogma,
but it understands love and sympathy.*

D. L. MOODY

APRIL 29

TRIED AND REFINED

You have tested us, O God; you have purified us like silver.

PSALM 66:10

In ancient times, a craftsman would refine silver by putting it in a cauldron and subjecting it to intense heat. As impurities rose to the surface of the boiling liquid, the craftsman would skim them away. Again and again he would repeat this process until the only thing visible on the surface of the silver was his own reflected image.

This is the word picture in Psalm 66. God subjects his people to various tests. These are not pleasant trials. But the end result is always something valuable and beautiful.

In short, God loves us too much to let us stay the way we are.

The power of the fire, we know, is twofold;
for it burns and it purifies; it burns what is corrupt;
but it purifies gold and silver from their dross.

JOHN CALVIN

UNITED IN CHRIST

*How wonderful and pleasant it is when
brothers live together in harmony!*

PSALM 133:1

Something isn't right. One of the background singers is off-key or pitchy—maybe even singing the wrong part. Instead of a pleasing harmony, the band suddenly sounds like a pack of coyotes howling at the moon.

In music—and in life—harmony is beautiful. In David's words, it's "wonderful and pleasant." But disharmony? Just the opposite! Sibling squabbles, church fights, warfare at work—such things are awful and unpleasant.

Unity doesn't mean uniformity. It means that different parts come together in a united way. We complement each other. We're for each other and pursuing the same goal. We see ourselves as allies instead of adversaries.

*If God be one, let all that profess him be of one
mind, and one heart, and thus fulfil Christ's
prayer, "that they all may be one."*

THOMAS WATSON

A HEAVY RESPONSIBILITY

Honor your father and mother. Then you will live a long, full life in the land the LORD your God is giving you.

EXODUS 20:12

Here's a verse for teens who are easily embarrassed by their parents. It's also pertinent for empty nesters with aging parents who need extra care. Since we all have parents, it's really a word for all of us.

The Hebrew word for *honor* is derived from the concept of heaviness or weightiness. The idea here is that parents should play a significant role and hold a special, important place in the lives of their children. For younger kids the priority is obedience. For older children it means showing parents genuine respect and treating them with dignity.

What do you think it looks like specifically and practically for you to honor your parents today?

Honor your parents and the Lord will honor you.

WOODROW KROLL

GET SOME REST!

On the seventh day God had finished his work
of creation, so he rested from all his work.

GENESIS 2:2

God *rested* from working? Is this a typo?

No. The Almighty rested after creating the universe, not because he was pooped out, but to signify that rest—rather than restlessness—is the goal of creation. In doing this, God built a work-rest rhythm into the very fabric of creation.

Think about it: crops go dormant. Animals hibernate. We need sleep every night. Rest is built into nature—and into *our* nature. We disregard this built-in rhythm at our own peril!

Of all the kinds of rest—physical, mental, emotional, spiritual—what kind do you feel the greatest need for today? What are ways the Lord might be providing that for you?

> *No soul can be really at rest until it has given*
> *up all dependence on everything else, and has*
> *been forced to depend on the Lord alone.*

HANNAH WHITALL SMITH

WHAT DO YOU LOVE?

*Wherever your treasure is, there the
desires of your heart will also be.*

MATTHEW 6:21

We humans are natural born treasure hunters—even if we don't all seek the same treasure.

One man values looks above all else. He devotes enormous chunks of time to dieting, working out with weights, and working on his tan. His sister values money. She pours herself into her lucrative career, then pores over the latest stock market returns.

Jesus explained that our hearts attach to whatever we deem most valuable and worthwhile in life. If you treasure love and companionship, you'll dream about meeting that special someone. If we treasure power, our hearts will scheme ways to get control over others. But if we treasure God above all else, our hearts will seek to show his love to others and bring his Kingdom about here on earth.

What do *you* love? Whatever you think, dream, and talk about most—that's your treasure.

*Give me five minutes with a person's checkbook,
and I will tell you where their heart is.*

BILLY GRAHAM

TRUE GOOD LOOKS

The LORD said to Samuel, "Don't judge by his appearance
or height, for I have rejected him. The LORD doesn't see
things the way you see them. People judge by outward
appearance, but the LORD looks at the heart.

1 SAMUEL 16:7

When Samuel showed up at Jesse's house to anoint a new king for Israel, he took one look at the oldest son and thought, *There's my guy.* A strapping, handsome young man, Eliab surely looked the part.

That's when God challenged his prophet—and us—with the words of this verse. We tend to make a big fuss over externals like smiles, good hair, and fabulous physiques. But God is all about internals—specifically, the heart.

Ask for the wisdom and grace to see beneath the surface in your interactions today.

Do not judge by appearances;
a rich heart may be under a poor coat.
SCOTTISH PROVERB

THE GREAT STORYTELLER

The LORD does whatever pleases him throughout all heaven and earth, and on the seas and in their depths.

PSALM 135:6

A bestselling novelist plots out her next book: how it will end, what will happen to all her characters. As she writes her story, her imagined creatures say and do things that she didn't consciously plan. They have real freedom—but within the limits of the narrative she has decided to tell.

This analogy illustrates the truth that God is the ultimate Author of life—and of our lives. We originated in the heart and mind of a great storyteller. Thus, as believers, we can trust that our lives and destinies really are in his big, good hands. Without a doubt, our story has an amazing ending.

Most Christians salute the sovereignty of God but believe in the sovereignty of man.

R. C. SPROUL

WOUNDS FROM A FRIEND

*Let the godly strike me! It will be a kindness! If they
correct me, it is soothing medicine. Don't let me refuse it.
But I pray constantly against the wicked and their deeds.*

PSALM 141:5

When someone confronts you about your behavior, do
you try to justify or rationalize your actions? Do you
change the subject, withdraw (either physically or emotionally), or counterattack? Or do you welcome such
confrontation as an opportunity to become better?

Notice that David viewed rebukes from his godly
friends as gifts of kindness. He saw corrective words as
healing medicine.

If we won't let others hold up a mirror to our souls,
if we balk when others speak into our lives, we will *never*
learn and grow. Ask God for the wisdom and courage to
hear the truth today.

*Truth demands confrontation; loving
confrontation, but confrontation nevertheless.*

FRANCIS A. SCHAEFFER

TO END ALL WARS

*The LORD will mediate between nations and will settle
international disputes. They will hammer their swords into
plowshares and their spears into pruning hooks. Nation will
no longer fight against nation, nor train for war anymore.*

ISAIAH 2:4

Scholars estimate that since about 1500 BC, the world
has experienced less than 275 years of global peace—
much of that enforced by Roman might. The number of
people that are thought to have perished in wars across
human history ranges from 150 million to one billion!

No wonder this verse is so beloved. Isaiah speaks of a
future day when the weapons of war will be turned into
farming implements. In short, a time is coming when
the world—under the Messiah's rule—will finally be at
peace.

Today, pray for peace in the world and live as a peacemaker in your home and community.

> *Lord, make me an instrument of your peace:
> where there is hatred, let me sow love.*
> FRANCIS OF ASSISI

HOW TO INHERIT A FORTUNE

God blesses those who are humble,
for they will inherit the whole earth.

MATTHEW 5:5

The distinguished estate attorney nods when asked about his latest succession. "It was sweet, ironic justice," he replies with a big smile. "The quiet, kind daughter, who clearly loved her millionaire dad more than she wanted any of his estate, got almost everything. Meanwhile, the loud, pushy, moneygrubbing daughter was cut out of the will."

Attention, credit, stuff, money, acclaim, recognition— proud people just want "theirs." But here the Lord says that those who humbly leave such "distributions" to God will, in the end, make out like bandits. They won't get just a few trinkets; they'll inherit the whole world.

Do you wish to rise? Begin by descending.
You plan a tower that will pierce the clouds?
Lay first the foundation of humility.

AUGUSTINE OF HIPPO

DRINKING SEAWATER

*On the last day, the climax of the festival, Jesus stood
and shouted to the crowds, "Anyone who is thirsty
may come to me! Anyone who believes in me may
come and drink! For the Scriptures declare, 'Rivers
of living water will flow from his heart.'"*

JOHN 7:37-38

Dying of thirst, the shipwreck survivors begin drinking
seawater, which only worsens their dehydration.

Here is a vivid (and grim) snapshot of humanity.
Shipwrecked by sin, we are *spiritually* thirsty. And even
though God is the only one who can satisfy us, we drink
up everything else the world has to offer. No wonder our
hearts are parched and cracked!

Read again the astonishing invitation of Jesus. Why
wouldn't you drink up his words, his very life?

*It is because Jesus Christ experienced cosmic thirst on the
cross that you and I can have our spiritual thirst satisfied.*

TIMOTHY KELLER

MORE THAN FOOD

*That is why I tell you not to worry about everyday
life—whether you have enough food and drink,
or enough clothes to wear. Isn't life more than
food, and your body more than clothing?*

MATTHEW 6:25

The flood victim looks at a lifetime of possessions—now
soggy and ruined—mounded up by the street. Yet she can
smile because her kids are safe and she has faith in a God
who promises to meet her needs.

She doesn't know where help will arise, only that
clothes and couches can be replaced. It's life that's
precious—and it's the hope of eternal life that keeps her
going through life's hard times.

Walk through your house. Thank God for providing you with so much—and thank him that life doesn't
depend on any of it.

*[Jesus] longs to relieve our worries and has promised
to supply our most fundamental needs.*
CHARLES R. SWINDOLL

GOD AND MONEY

*Honor the LORD with your wealth and with the best part
of everything you produce. Then he will fill your barns
with grain, and your vats will overflow with good wine.*

PROVERBS 3:9-10

Honoring the Lord with our money can feel vague and abstract. But we can draw on biblical principles to understand this proverbial word.

We should begin by *recognizing* God as the source of everything—all our aptitudes, talents, and opportunities for learning and earning. We should be quick in *thanking* him for all the blessings he has given us. We must get in the habit of *giving* generously—not because God needs our donations but to make much of him and also to loosen our grip on money before it grips our hearts. Ultimately, we will learn to *trust* him (and not our financial assets) as we live day to day.

Pick one concrete way you can honor God with your wealth today, and do it.

*The most obvious lesson in Christ's teaching is that there is no
happiness in having and getting anything, but only in giving.*

HENRY DRUMMOND

BACK FROM THE FUTURE

How do you know what your life will be like tomorrow?
Your life is like the morning fog—it's here a little
while, then it's gone. What you ought to say is, "If the
Lord wants us to, we will live and do this or that."

JAMES 4:14-15

Tom is—and isn't—on vacation with his family. Oh, his body is at the beach, but his mind is already living *next week*, alternately scheming and worrying about upcoming events. Every minute he spends fretting over the future is a minute he's not present for his actual life.

James condemns such presumptive thinking. First, we're not all-knowing. Our planning only amounts to conjecture. Second, life is short enough without us frittering away our time in fantasyland. Third, God controls our futures.

How about today we live for today?

He that fears not the future may enjoy the present.
THOMAS FULLER

MAY 13

UNDER NEW OWNERSHIP

*Don't you realize that your body is the temple of
the Holy Spirit, who lives in you and was given to
you by God? You do not belong to yourself.*

1 CORINTHIANS 6:19

Culture says your body is yours to do with as you please.
Care for it or neglect it—it's your choice. Indulge it or
discipline it. Starve it or overfeed it. Wear it out. Decorate
it. When it comes to sex, do whatever you want.

The biblical view says that our bodies—not just our
souls—belong to the Lord. At salvation, the Holy Spirit
joined believers to Christ *and* took up residence in us.
Therefore, we should dedicate our bodies to God's purposes and his glory.

How can you more fully devote your body to God
today?

*Never tell a child, "You have a soul." Teach him,
you are a soul; you have a body.*
GEORGE MACDONALD

MAY 14

LAYING IT DOWN

---

*There is no greater love than to lay
down one's life for one's friends.*

JOHN 15:13

Less than twenty-four hours after saying this, Jesus lived his words. He allowed Roman soldiers to hammer his battered body to a cross. He died so his followers wouldn't have to.

Jesus is the ultimate example of "laying down one's life." But there are other ways we can show love for others. We can lay down our rights, our desires, our demands, and our pride. We can lay down our selfishness. We can put to death our resentment and our bitterness. Maybe it's an agenda or a dream that we need to lay down.

The point is, love sacrifices. It surrenders. What are some ways that you can self-sacrificially love others today?

*The best use of life is love. The best expression of
love is time. The best time to love is now.*

RICK WARREN

IN ENEMY TERRITORY

*Dear friends, I warn you as "temporary residents
and foreigners" to keep away from worldly desires
that wage war against your very souls.*

1 PETER 2:11

At least two powerful spiritual truths about the world are
conveyed in this short verse:

> *This world isn't our home.* We're temporary residents
> whose permanent address is heaven.
>
> *This world is dangerous.* It's filled with sinful
> temptations that function like land mines in
> the great cosmic spiritual war that is ongoing
> all around us.

The implications are clear: as believers we need to
focus less on being *comfortable* and more on being *careful*.
Carelessness will make us casualties!

What worldly desires pose the biggest danger to your
own heart right now?

*If you turn your back on the greatness and majesty of God,
you'll fall in love with a world of shadows and short-lived pleasures.*

JOHN PIPER

GOD OF THE WEAK

Father to the fatherless, defender of widows—
this is God, whose dwelling is holy.

PSALM 68:5

Our culture is captivated by attractive and charismatic people. If you're pretty or powerful, talented or outrageous, you can have millions of followers on social media—and maybe even your own reality TV show.

Our God, meanwhile, is drawn to the downtrodden. If you're an orphan or a widow on a fixed income, if you're poor or friendless, if you're incapacitated or incarcerated, you can find help and hope in the Almighty. He happily draws near to those who humbly draw near to him (see James 4:6-8).

Today's verse reminds us that God cares for those who have been abandoned or hurt in this life. When we experience the troubles of this world, we can have faith that God will meet us there.

His is a loving, tender hand, full of sympathy and compassion.
D. L. MOODY

AN ATTEMPT TO TEMPT

Keep watch and pray, so that you will not give in to temptation. For the spirit is willing, but the body is weak!

MATTHEW 26:41

God referred to the nation of Israel as "my firstborn son" (Exodus 4:22) and "my servant" (Isaiah 44:21). But Israel was a disobedient son and an unfaithful servant from the very outset. When tempted in the wilderness, the people of Israel rebelled against God's commandments.

This is why Jesus' victory over sin and Satan in the wilderness is such a big deal. He is the obedient Son and faithful Servant of God! In times of temptation, he honored and submitted to God's Word! And so in today's passage, Jesus' example of resisting temptation teaches us to heed the same warning he gave his disciples in his final hours.

Today, when you're tempted, remember Jesus' spiritual tenacity. Ask him for strength as you stand upon his Word.

Temptations and occasions put nothing into a man, but only draw out what was in him before.

JOHN OWEN

SERVING LIKE THE SAVIOR

Even the Son of Man came not to be served but to serve others and to give his life as a ransom for many.

MARK 10:45

Here's the verse that best summarizes the extraordinary life of Jesus. God became man in order to serve and save humankind.

In his brief ministry, Jesus taught God's truth, healed the sick, fed the hungry masses, encouraged the downcast, washed dirty feet, and gave dignity to women, children, and other social outcasts.

Jesus served the Father perfectly by living to serve others and, in the end, dying to save others.

If you want a model for how the Christian life was meant to be lived, there it is.

Since [God] is invisible to our eyes, we are to serve Him in our neighbor: which He receives as if done to Himself in person, standing visibly before us.

JOHN WESLEY

CROWD OF WITNESSES

*Since we are surrounded by such a huge crowd of witnesses
to the life of faith, let us strip off every weight that slows us
down, especially the sin that so easily trips us up. And let
us run with endurance the race God has set before us.*

HEBREWS 12:1

Some think this verse depicts all the saints in heaven
watching and cheering the exploits of believers on
earth—much like spectators in a giant stadium.

The verse more likely means that given our great
legacy of faith (i.e., all the faithful believers mentioned
in Hebrews 11), let's be strong in faith too. Let's stop sinning and start running all out for God, all the way home.

What's slowing you down today? Lay it aside and run!

*The only way to learn strong faith is to endure great trials.
I have learned my faith by standing firm amid severe testings.*

GEORGE MÜLLER

PARTNERS WITH GOD

*Because of his glory and excellence, he has given us
great and precious promises. These are the promises
that enable you to share his divine nature and escape
the world's corruption caused by human desires.*

2 PETER 1:4

Here's the famous verse that says believers share God's divine nature. What on earth does that mean?

When we are "born again" (John 3:3), we become new creatures (see 2 Corinthians 5:17)—"children of God" (John 1:12), indwelt by the very Spirit of God (Romans 8:9). We don't become divine, but it's as though God's DNA is implanted within us.

In the place of death, we receive life—God's life. In the place of old habits and tendencies, we receive a new nature, new desires, new power, and a new calling. The only question: Will we choose to go God's new way?

There is no escape from the need to depend on God's grace.

JAMES BOICE

RETURN TO ME

Say to the people, "This is what the LORD of Heaven's
Armies says: Return to me, and I will return to
you, says the LORD of Heaven's Armies."

ZECHARIAH 1:3

To the spiritually wandering Jews who had returned to
Israel from seven decades of Babylonian captivity, God
commanded, "Return to me" (alternatively, "repent").

This is a gracious invitation, not an angry denunciation. *Repent*, a misunderstood word so disliked by many
people, can be translated "turn back," "come back," or
"go back." And what's the goal of all that backtracking?
Restoration and refreshment.

Maybe you're wandering away from your faith today.
Perhaps you feel unmotivated or disinterested or down-
right distracted. The Lord's command to you is the same
one he gave the exiles: "Return to me."

What will you get if you do?

Him!

Repentance, as we know, is basically not moaning
and remorse, but turning and change.

J. I. PACKER

A GREAT REWARD

*God blesses you when people mock you and persecute you
and lie about you and say all sorts of evil things against you
because you are my followers. Be happy about it! Be very glad!
For a great reward awaits you in heaven. And remember,
the ancient prophets were persecuted in the same way.*

MATTHEW 5:11-12

Jesus promises us that we will face persecution for following him. He also assures us that we are in good company—generations of faithful saints have gone before us.

When we are mocked and ridiculed, we might not feel like smiling, but we do have reason to. When you are persecuted, look to Jesus. A great reward is waiting for you.

*Joy flows in the night as well as in the day; joy flows all
through persecution and opposition; it flows right along,
for it is an unceasing fountain bubbling up in the heart.*

D. L. MOODY

BORN TWICE

*Jesus replied, "I tell you the truth, unless you are born
again, you cannot see the Kingdom of God."*

JOHN 3:3

Wouldn't you love to see a video of this moment? The
look on Nicodemus's face? How long he paused before
responding to Jesus?

If anyone was ever seemingly perfect for the Kingdom
of God, it was Nicodemus. His religious résumé was
impeccable: "a Jewish religious leader who was a Pharisee"
(John 3:1); "a respected Jewish teacher" (John 3:10).

But Jesus said that none of this is enough. Entering
God's Kingdom requires being "born again." In short,
before we try to live a new life *for* God, we first need new
life *from* God.

If you're not sure that you have come alive spiritually,
ask God for new life today.

*Continue seeking [God] with seriousness. Unless He
wanted you, you would not be wanting Him.*

C. S. LEWIS

TRY IT YOURSELF AND SEE

I have been a constant example of how you can help those in need by working hard. You should remember the words of the Lord Jesus: "It is more blessed to give than to receive."

ACTS 20:35

In saying farewell to his Ephesian friends, Paul mentioned his habit of helping those in need. He then quoted this statement of Jesus that's not found in the Gospels: "It is more blessed to give than to receive."

What? We get more by *giving* more—not by *getting* more? Really? That sounds so counterintuitive.

Maybe our giving leads to instantaneous spiritual and emotional satisfaction. Or maybe we receive the promised blessing later. Whatever the case, the only way to know *by experience* that Jesus' words are true is to try them yourself and see.

Help one person at a time and always start with the person nearest you.

MOTHER TERESA

THE GOOD SHEPHERD

I am the good shepherd. The good shepherd
sacrifices his life for the sheep.

JOHN 10:11

In Jesus' day, there were a lot of shady shepherds. It's possible people made cracks about them the way modern-day people joke about lawyers, politicians, IRS agents, and TV evangelists.

To complicate matters, many shepherds didn't actually own the flocks in their care. Shepherding was just a job—a way to earn a living. This meant that these hired hands weren't terribly motivated, especially when a predator attacked or a sheep got lost.

Jesus is the antithesis of a sketchy, indifferent shepherd. He's good. He *loves* his sheep. How can we be sure? Because when his flock faced eternal danger, he died to save them.

God . . . never abandons anyone on whom he has set his love;
nor does Christ, the good shepherd, ever lose track of his sheep.

J. I. PACKER

PURE TRUST

It is impossible to please God without faith. Anyone
who wants to come to him must believe that God exists
and that he rewards those who sincerely seek him.

HEBREWS 11:6

A severe drought prompted a Midwestern farming community to call an emergency prayer meeting. Among those who gathered to appeal to the Almighty for rain was a five-year-old girl—doll in one hand, umbrella in the other. As the adults prayed fervently, the child gazed expectantly into the evening sky.

This kind of faith pleases God—not a demanding spirit, but a settled assurance that God hears the prayers of his people. Faith doesn't only talk; it also takes action. It's not crossing one's fingers and hoping for the best. Faith is counting on God to come through.

What need are you trusting God to meet today?

Cleverness is cheap. It is the faith he praises.
GEORGE MACDONALD

THE ULTIMATE SOURCE OF TRUTH

A time is coming when people will no longer listen to sound and wholesome teaching. They will follow their own desires and will look for teachers who will tell them whatever their itching ears want to hear.

2 TIMOTHY 4:3

Paul wrote, "A time is coming." We might well think, "The time is here." You probably know people who are only interested in teachers who say what they want to hear. Maybe that describes you.

But this kind of teaching does nothing good. False teachings may make us feel smug, but they will only hurt us in the long run.

So how do we know if a teaching is true? We must compare it to God's Word. We must verify it against the ultimate source of truth.

So few grow because so few study.

D. L. MOODY

ETERNAL CONSISTENCY

I am the LORD, and I do not change.

MALACHI 3:6

What a day, Stephanie thinks as she slides wearily into bed.

During her commute, her best friend called to reveal she's moving next month. This afternoon, HR sent an e-mail about a 25 percent increase in employee health care premiums for next year. To cap off a day of bad news, her ex-husband texted tonight to say he wants to amend their child custody agreement. Staring at the dark ceiling, Stephanie feels untethered, like her life is spinning out of control.

She needs the reminder of this verse, and maybe you do too: in a world where people, institutions, and situations change *constantly*, God is forever the same. He alone is our rock.

He cannot change for the better, for He is already perfect;
and being perfect, He cannot change for the worse.

A. W. PINK

LYRICS OF LOVE

No power in the sky above or in the earth below—indeed,
nothing in all creation will ever be able to separate us from
the love of God that is revealed in Christ Jesus our Lord.

ROMANS 8:39

Think of the best love song you've ever heard, that heart-tugging declaration of all-consuming passion. Now realize even *that* song's affectionate lyrics can't compare with this immortal verse. Ponder Paul's inspired words carefully.

"No power . . . nothing in all creation"—that is, nothing and no one in all the universe—"will ever be able to separate us from the love of God." How's that for absolute and unconditional and permanent?

How differently would you live your life if you believed to the core of your being that you are, now and forever, cherished and adored by God?

Define yourself radically as one beloved by
God. . . . Every other identity is illusion.
BRENNAN MANNING

TOP PRIORITY

We tell others about Christ, warning everyone and teaching
everyone with all the wisdom God has given us. We want to
present them to God, perfect in their relationship to Christ.

COLOSSIANS 1:28

The goal of the Christian life isn't to acquire biblical trivia
or to have epic spiritual experiences. It surely isn't to "get
busy serving God."

Following Jesus is an event; it's *coming to* Christ by
faith, followed by a lifelong process of *becoming like* him.

This mind-set shaped Paul's ministry. He *told others*
about Christ, then *warned* (alternatively, *counseled*) and
taught them. He passed on all the truth God revealed to
him. And why? So that people might be "perfect" (i.e.,
mature) in Christ. Christlikeness is the goal.

Where is that happening in your life? Where does it
still need to happen?

Growth [is] the only evidence of life.
THOMAS SCOTT OF ASTON SANDFORD

THE BOTTOM LINE

That's the whole story. Here now is my final conclusion:
Fear God and obey his commands, for this is everyone's
duty. God will judge us for everything we do,
including every secret thing, whether good or bad.

ECCLESIASTES 12:13-14

Ecclesiastes reads like the journal of a cynical, world-weary man (probably because it is). Solomon documented his futile search for satisfaction. Nothing—not education, pleasure, or achievement—could fill the hole in his soul.

At the end of his search, Solomon admitted that apart from a relationship with the living God, life is utterly empty.

Some people could hear that testimony a thousand times and still not be convinced. The wise, however, learn from the experiences—good and bad—of others. May we be among the wise.

As all the rivers are gathered into the ocean, so Christ is
the ocean in which all true delights and pleasures meet.

JOHN FLAVEL

IDENTITY AND CALLING

*After his baptism, as Jesus came up out of the water, the
heavens were opened and he saw the Spirit of God descending
like a dove and settling on him. And a voice from heaven
said, "This is my dearly loved Son, who brings me great joy."*

MATTHEW 3:16-17

There's so much in this familiar passage. Historically,
it marks the beginning of Christ's earthly ministry.
Theologically, it touches on baptism and the Trinity.
Personally and spiritually, it reveals the stunning relationship between God the Father and Jesus, his Son.

The Father "dearly *loves*" the Son. The Son brings the
Father "great joy."

This is the model for every child of God: first realize
how much God delights in you; then desire to live to
delight him.

*The greatest honor we can give Almighty God is to
live gladly because of the knowledge of his love.*

JULIAN OF NORWICH

WHAT GOD HAS JOINED TOGETHER

"Haven't you read the Scriptures?" Jesus replied. "They record that from the beginning 'God made them male and female.'" And he said, "'This explains why a man leaves his father and mother and is joined to his wife, and the two are united into one.' Since they are no longer two but one, let no one split apart what God has joined together."

MATTHEW 19:4-6

The Pharisees questioned Jesus about marriage, and Jesus answered them by quoting the Old Testament. Jesus told them that, long before, God had designed marriage to be a powerful thing: two individuals coming together to become something new, a partnership that brings glory to God.

This doesn't mean that marriage will be easy. But it does mean that marriage matters to God, and that he cares about what happens within each one.

As God by creation made two of one, so again by marriage He made one of two.

THOMAS ADAMS

CALLED TO SINGLEHOOD

I wish everyone were single, just as I am. Yet each person
has a special gift from God, of one kind or another.
So I say to those who aren't married and to widows—
it's better to stay unmarried, just as I am.

1 CORINTHIANS 7:7-8

Not everyone is called to marriage, and these verses have
encouraged countless single saints.

Singlehood has enabled many people to accomplish
great things for God. Patricia Green founded ministries
to help victims of human trafficking. Gladys Aylward
saved the lives of countless orphans in China. Paul chose
to remain single, because he wanted to invest all his
energy in the work of God.

Marriage isn't wrong. Singlehood isn't wrong. God
calls people to different lives for different reasons.
Whatever he's called you to, he will help you to do his
good work.

The gift of singleness is more a vocation than
an empowerment, although to be sure God is
faithful in supporting those He calls.

JOHN R. W. STOTT

THE BOY JESUS

---

*Jesus grew in wisdom and in stature and in
favor with God and all the people.*

LUKE 2:52

We have very few details about Jesus' childhood: the
beloved Christmas story told in Matthew and Luke, the
account of his family's escape to Egypt, the anecdote of
him dialoguing with the scribes at the Temple when he
was twelve. That's it—except for this verse.

Here Luke shows us Jesus' full humanity. While he
developed physically ("in stature"), he also grew "in wisdom" and "in favor with God and . . . people."

This verse is a handy checklist for a life that honors
God. Ask yourself these questions: Am I growing wiser in
making decisions? What am I doing to stay healthy? How
can I improve my relationships with God and others?

All growth that is not towards God is growing to decay.
GEORGE MACDONALD

NAME-CALLING

See how very much our Father loves us, for he calls us his children, and that is what we are! But the people who belong to this world don't recognize that we are God's children because they don't know him.

1 JOHN 3:1

The world calls Christians all sorts of names, including "freaks," "weirdos," "wackos," and "Bible thumpers."

God's Word calls believers "saints," "conquerors," "citizens of heaven," "salt," "light," and (according to this astonishing verse) "God's children."

It might sound crazy, but "that is what we are!" When you believe and accept Christ, God gives you the right to become his child (John 1:12). Think of that: he loved you enough to adopt you through Jesus!

Ignore the name-calling. Who in your life needs to hear this good news?

If anybody understands God's ardor for his children, it's someone who has rescued an orphan from despair, for that is what God has done for us.

MAX LUCADO

A NEW CALLING

Jesus called out to them, "Come, follow me,
and I will show you how to fish for people!"

MARK 1:17

We often ask people about their *jobs* and tell them about our *work*. But long before all this talk of professions and careers, people used to speak of their *vocations* (from a Latin word that means "calling").

In this famous verse we see Jesus calling Andrew and Peter to be his disciples. Their previous job was catching fish. Their new vocation would be to learn how to fish for people.

In a real sense, that's every Christian's calling: to follow Jesus and learn how to catch people for him. If that analogy seems cold or manipulative to you, remember this: the net we cast is the ultimate safety net.

Come you and follow Christ for the sake
of what he can make out of you.
CHARLES SPURGEON

THE ONE AND ONLY YOU

Thank you for making me so wonderfully complex! Your workmanship is marvelous—how well I know it.

PSALM 139:14

Few people look in the mirror and love everything they see. Usually it's: *I'm overweight!* Or *I hate my hair.* Or *Why do I have to be so short?* Often we do the same with abilities: *If only I could* _____. Contrast these self-critical thoughts with David's realization.

Each of us is an original masterpiece. That's because our God is not into cloning. No one else has (or has had or will have) your unique combination of skills and smarts, looks and lacks.

By faith, thank God for all your strengths and shortcomings. Your strengths can make you a blessing to others. Your weaknesses open the door for others to bless you.

God . . . knit you together within the womb;
you're just what He wanted to make.

RUSSELL KELFER

GOD IN A BOX

"My thoughts are nothing like your thoughts," says the LORD.
"And my ways are far beyond anything you could imagine."

ISAIAH 55:8

Someone who tries to put God in a box arrogantly predicts—or worse, dictates—exactly what the Almighty will do about a situation and how (or even when) he will do it.

To be sure, God reveals much about his nature in the Bible. He gives us promises we can rely on. Consequently, we *can* know and trust him. But his timing isn't at all predictable. And the means he uses to accomplish his will are almost always surprising.

The point is this: if you, with your finite mind, think you've got the infinite God all figured out, that's a sure sign you don't. Trust that he knows what he's doing in your life.

God moves in a mysterious way, His wonders to perform.
WILLIAM COWPER

OUR STEPS

We can make our plans, but the LORD determines our steps.

PROVERBS 16:9

Robert Burns wrote, "The best laid schemes o' Mice an' Men [often go awry]." We are a little like mice in that, no matter how well we plan, ultimately, we are not in control of how those plans turn out. But that's okay as long as we know and trust the one who *is* in control.

It's good to plan, to make goals, and to work to achieve those goals, as long as we remain obedient to God in the steps we take toward our goals. If we surrender to God in the details, we will likely end up thrilled at just how fabulously things turn out.

If men make God's glory their end, and his will their rule, he will direct their steps by his Spirit and grace.
MATTHEW HENRY

MERCY YIELDS MERCY

God blesses those who are merciful,
for they will be shown mercy.

MATTHEW 5:7

In a dog-eat-dog world, it seems nobody's giving out awards for mercy. Sadly, many people view showing mercy as weakness at best, idiocy at worst. They say, "Don't help those who hurt you; seek revenge. Don't take time from your busy life to show compassion to people in need; they'll just take advantage of you."

Jesus plays by totally different rules. In his Kingdom, the merciful are heroes who show incredible strength of character. Their acts of kindness don't lead to self-deprivation. On the contrary, merciful people receive the blessing of a lifetime, an all-you-need supply of mercy.

God knows we need that. And we get it by showing it!

The most miserable prison in the world is the prison we
make for ourselves when we refuse to show mercy.

WARREN WIERSBE

DRIVING OUT DARKNESS

Jesus spoke to the people once more and said, "I am the light of the world. If you follow me, you won't have to walk in darkness, because you will have the light that leads to life."

JOHN 8:12

Play the word association game and say, "Darkness." You might hear people respond with words like *danger*, *sin*, *crime*, or *fear*.

Throughout the Bible, *darkness* is used to describe spiritual blindness, wickedness, hatred, captivity, death, destruction, calamity, and fear—all the result of sinfulness in our world (see Psalm 107:14; Proverbs 4:19; Matthew 6:23; Romans 2:19; 1 John 2:9; Revelation 16:10).

Thankfully, Jesus is the light of the world. When we walk with him, we have nothing to fear, we are never lost, and we are never in ultimate danger.

Darkness cannot drive out darkness; only light can do that. Hate cannot drive out hate; only love can do that.

MARTIN LUTHER KING JR.

THE GREAT REVERSAL

*Seek the Kingdom of God above all else, and live
righteously, and he will give you everything you need.*

MATTHEW 6:33

Many people reason, "Once I get everything I want and
need in life—a spouse, a house, a good career, and a secure
financial situation—*then* I will get serious about God."

According to Jesus, this type of reasoning is back-
ward. Our top priority in life should be to righteously
pursue what God wants for our lives and trust his leading.

Wrestle today with these two questions:

1. What would it look like—practically and
   specifically—for me to "seek the Kingdom
   of God above all else"?
2. Do I truly believe that God will give me
   everything I need if I seek him first?

*If you have not chosen the Kingdom of God first, it will in
the end make no difference what you have chosen instead.*

WILLIAM LAW

RIGHT HERE

*I can never escape from your Spirit! I can never get
away from your presence! If I go up to heaven, you
are there; if I go down to the grave, you are there.*

PSALM 139:7-8

God is everywhere. We can't evade him, no matter how
hard we try, no matter where we go. And we know from
the New Testament that the Lord is not just *with* his
people; he's *in* us, by his Spirit.

The Creator is present with you right now, closer
than you can possibly fathom. Instead of saying, "Lord,
be with me today," pray, "Thank you, Lord, for being
with me." What we need isn't the *presence* of God—we
have that already—but the *awareness* of his presence.

*I must first have the sense of God's possession of me
before I can have the sense of his presence with me.*

WATCHMAN NEE

CONFESSION'S HEALING POWER

Confess your sins to each other and pray for each other so that you may be healed. The earnest prayer of a righteous person has great power and produces wonderful results.

JAMES 5:16

You'll sometimes hear recovering alcoholics say, "You're only as sick as your secrets."

What they know—usually from years of misery—is that hiding our failures from others is the surest way to stay enslaved in destructive habits. True freedom, on the other hand, begins the day we come clean and openly admit our struggles.

This is James's point here. Bible readers who get hung up on whether he's referring to physical or spiritual healing should remember that healing is the by-product; confession is the point.

Whom can you share your struggle with today? Take that first step toward healing and freedom.

There are many that blush to confess their faults, who never blush to commit them.

WILLIAM SECKER

JUNE 15

SHOW AND TELL

---

*You must worship Christ as Lord of your life.
And if someone asks about your hope as a
believer, always be ready to explain it.*

1 PETER 3:15

Some see evangelism as an either-or situation: we either show our faith by living an exemplary life, or we tell others about our faith every chance we get.

The apostle Peter said it's a both-and scenario. Let Jesus control your life, *and* also explain to curious neighbors and coworkers what makes you different.

Be a show-and-tell disciple today. Live an attractive life that causes people to ask questions. Then use your lips to give the reasons for your hope.

*Make up your mind to do whatever you can to
help your friends and acquaintances come to
know and cherish the Savior. He's a wonderful,
magnificent, glorious, loving Lord, and he's
asking you to join him in his harvest field.*

JOSEPH ALDRICH

YOUR CHEATING HEART

The human heart is the most deceitful of all things,
and desperately wicked. Who really knows how bad
it is? But I, the LORD, search all hearts and examine
secret motives. I give all people their due rewards,
according to what their actions deserve.

JEREMIAH 17:9-10

Here's the story of the world in a nutshell: humanity was created *by* God for happiness *in* God. However, this plan was promptly ruined when the first humans believed the devilish lie that they could find happiness *outside of* God.

Ever since, human nature has been deplorable. People lie, manipulate, betray, cheat, steal, and kill to try to get whatever they think will make them happy.

The situation would be beyond bleak, except that God sees and understands all the mixed-up, messed-up motives in our hearts. And he has the power to transform us through Christ.

[God] sees hearts as we see faces.
GEORGE HERBERT

JUNE 17

OUR ADVOCATE

My dear children, I am writing this to you so that
you will not sin. But if anyone does sin, we have
an advocate who pleads our case before the Father.
He is Jesus Christ, the one who is truly righteous.

1 JOHN 2:1

Those in trouble want a top-notch defense attorney standing beside them in court, someone who will know every law, precedent, loophole, and technicality. Hire the best and you'll never even have to take the stand!

This is a picture of Jesus, the perfect "advocate who pleads our case before the Father."

"Don't sin—at all!" John warns. "However, if you do, don't despair. Jesus Christ was convicted so you could be exonerated! He's your airtight defense!"

No sin is small. It is a sin against an infinite God,
and may have consequences immeasurable. No grain
of sand is small in the mechanism of a watch.

JEREMY TAYLOR

JUNE 18

FOR SUCH A TIME AS THIS

If you keep quiet at a time like this, deliverance and
relief for the Jews will arise from some other place, but
you and your relatives will die. Who knows if perhaps
you were made queen for just such a time as this?

ESTHER 4:14

Around 478 BC, a gorgeous Jewish girl named Esther
unexpectedly became the queen of Persia. Soon after,
when a genocidal plot arose against the Jews living in
exile there, Esther's relative Mordecai spoke these famous
words to her.

Mordecai was basically saying, "Do you think your
beauty and position of influence are accidental? In this
crucial moment, will you choose to make a difference?"

Why did God give *you* the things you have? And how
will you use all that for his glory?

Do good: as we have time, and opportunity, to do good in
every possible kind, and in every possible degree to all men.

JOHN WESLEY

DARK BEFORE THE DAWN

---

*His anger lasts only a moment, but his favor
lasts a lifetime! Weeping may last through the
night, but joy comes with the morning.*

PSALM 30:5

In this beloved psalm, David mentions needing rescue
from enemies (verse 1), crying out for help (verse 2), and
being near death (verses 3, 9). While we don't know the
exact context surrounding the writing of this psalm, these
details provide some clues about the depth of turmoil
David was experiencing in his life.

As a result of some kind of divine discipline or
worldly trial, David was suffering enough to weep bit-
terly and pray desperately for mercy.

Maybe you've been there. Maybe you *are* there.

Be encouraged. David's darkness lifted; hope
returned. He was able to sing, "Joy comes with the morning." God can do that for you, too.

It is always darkest just before the Day dawneth.
THOMAS FULLER

THE WALKING DEAD

God is so rich in mercy, and he loved us so much,
that even though we were dead because of our sins,
he gave us life when he raised Christ from the dead.
(It is only by God's grace that you have been saved!)

EPHESIANS 2:4-5

First Hollywood discovered vampires. Then the focus switched to zombies. The zombie narrative usually goes like this: people are infected with a mystery virus, die, and then reanimate into mindless creatures that roam about and make trouble.

In the Bible, unbelievers are described in zombie-like terms. The deadly virus that afflicts them is sin. Though physically alive, those outside of Christ are said to be spiritually and morally dead. They walk (see Ephesians 2:2, NASB) about, animated by the evil one.

In the movies and TV shows, there's no hope for zombies. Their curse is to wander lifelessly, presumably forever, or they are killed. The gospel, however, says the walking dead can be made alive by Christ.

This amazing love of God . . . gave us life when
we were dead, and caused us to be born again,
and brought us into the family of God.

JOHN PIPER

DISCERNING WHAT'S TRUE

When the Spirit of truth comes, he will guide you into all truth. He will not speak on his own but will tell you what he has heard. He will tell you about the future.

JOHN 16:13

With countless so-called experts making contradictory truth claims, this is a wonderful promise from Christ.

About seven weeks after Jesus promised to send his followers the Spirit of truth, the Holy Spirit came into the lives of believers (see Acts 2).

One of the Spirit's primary ministries is to guide believers into all truth. At the very least, this means when we hear things that sound contrary to biblical teaching, we can consult God's Spirit. He will tell us if what we're hearing is absolutely true or utterly false.

We should note this curious mark of our age:
The only absolute allowed is the absolute
insistence that there is no absolute.

FRANCIS A. SCHAEFFER

WHEN YOU'RE SINKING

Answer my prayers, O LORD, for your unfailing
love is wonderful. Take care of me, for your mercy
is so plentiful. Don't hide from your servant;
answer me quickly, for I am in deep trouble!

PSALM 69:16-17

Two things are true of the anguished prayers categorized
as the psalms of lament: they are brutally authentic and
stubbornly God-focused.

In Psalm 69, David is in a serious mess. He doesn't
pretend everything is fine. He admits to being weary and
scared, frustrated and humiliated. Simultaneously, he
clings and cries, pleads and prays relentlessly. God is his
only hope.

Are *you* going under? Follow David's lead. Call to the
one who is able to save.

Pray until you can pray. Pray to be helped to pray, and do
not give up praying because you cannot pray. It is when
you think you cannot pray that you are most praying.

CHARLES H. SPURGEON

NO FEAR—HE'S HERE

They were all terrified when they saw him.
But Jesus spoke to them at once. "Don't be afraid,"
he said. "Take courage! I am here!"

MARK 6:50

The divine command "Don't be afraid" (and its assorted variations) is found more than one hundred times in the Bible.

Surely the reason the Lord repeated this so often to his people is that we have a natural tendency toward panic and dread. Experience confirms that we start to freak out the moment we forget his presence, power, and promises.

Here Jesus, out for a midnight stroll on the Sea of Galilee, reassures his terrified disciples and gives them the opportunity to respond. In most life situations, we face a similar choice: faith or fear.

He that has his trust set upon God does not need to dread
anything except the weakening or the paralysing of that trust.
ALEXANDER MACLAREN

LIVING WORDS

The word of God is alive and powerful. It is sharper
than the sharpest two-edged sword, cutting between
soul and spirit, between joint and marrow. It
exposes our innermost thoughts and desires.

HEBREWS 4:12

People speak of Bible verses jumping off the page. Or
they talk of their hearts being pierced by a biblical truth
they'd never grasped before.

Perhaps you've had a similar experience. You've felt
overwhelming peace while pondering a divine promise.

All these expressions are ways of referring to the
dynamic nature of Scripture. And we shouldn't be sur-
prised. After all, we are talking about the eternal Word
of our all-powerful, good God.

Ask God for a heart that hungers to hear his voice—
and for ears to hear it.

The Bible is alive, it speaks to me; it has feet, it
runs after me; it has hands, it lays hold of me.

MARTIN LUTHER

FULLY DRESSED IN HUMILITY

All of you, dress yourselves in humility as you relate to one another, for "God opposes the proud but gives grace to the humble." So humble yourselves under the mighty power of God, and at the right time he will lift you up in honor.

1 PETER 5:5-6

It has been said that "clothes make the man." And often, the first thing we notice about another person is what they are wearing.

Peter encourages us here to dress ourselves in humility. This means that humility is something we want people to notice about us, a distinction that makes our submission to God plain to others. Pride draws a lot of attention—but clearly it's not a good kind of attention.

Pride tells others to look at us, but humility has a way of pointing others to God whenever they see it on us. Today, examine how you are still struggling to give up your pride, and pray for humility to grow in your life.

You can have no greater sign of a more confirmed pride, than when you think that you are humble enough.

WILLIAM LAW

WHAT'S IMPORTANT?

*Many who are the greatest now will be least
important then, and those who seem least
important now will be the greatest then.*

MARK 10:31

What makes a person great? A net worth of $75 billion?
Having 90 million followers on Twitter? Making it on
People magazine's annual "Most Beautiful" list? Being a
household name?

According to Jesus, these sorts of accomplishments
won't matter in heaven. Greatness requires a willingness
to serve others: the gentle nurse's aide who shows Christ's
love to nursing home residents; the single working mom
who sacrificially raises her kids; the meticulous Bible
translator who labors in obscurity to make God's Word
available to an unreached people group. These are the
ones who will receive recognition in heaven.

How encouraging is *that*? You don't have to be "great"
to be truly great!

Those who think too much of themselves don't think enough.

AMY CARMICHAEL

WAKE UP!

Be on your guard, not asleep like the others.
Stay alert and be clearheaded.

1 THESSALONIANS 5:6

The Wizard of Oz features that unforgettable scene in which Dorothy and her fellow travelers come to a large poppy field, forget their quest, and fall into a trance-like sleep.

The lesson? Complacency is dangerous! In seeking the Kingdom of God, we can become weary. *What would it hurt to take a break?* we reason. Soon we are snoring—not the normal, necessary rest that God wants for all his people, but an extended, coma-like unconsciousness.

Trapped in this lethargic, drowsy mind-set, it's possible to sleepwalk for long stretches of life. No wonder God's word to his people is "Awake, O sleeper" (Ephesians 5:14).

But he who would be born again indeed,
must wake his soul unnumbered times a day,
and urge himself to life with holy greed.

GEORGE MACDONALD

CULTIVATING THANKFULNESS

Be thankful in all circumstances, for this is God's will for you who belong to Christ Jesus.

1 THESSALONIANS 5:18

Feeling appreciative for blessings is easy. Even well-mannered pagans do that. But Paul's command here is to be thankful in *all* circumstances—not just in good times, but in bad times too.

This makes zero sense unless we believe that God's heart is good and that he is wisely orchestrating all the details of our lives. Consider this: maybe that flat tire kept you from being broadsided by a drunk driver. Or maybe that pay cut is God's mercy—a way of getting you to address some deep heart issues.

Pray for the grace to trust that God is in control—even in unpleasant times. Cultivate the habit of thanking him, by faith, for whatever comes.

The beginning of man's rebellion against God was, and is, the lack of a thankful heart.

FRANCIS A. SCHAEFFER

INCOMPREHENSIBLE

*May you experience the love of Christ, though it is too great
to understand fully. Then you will be made complete with
all the fullness of life and power that comes from God.*

EPHESIANS 3:19

An excited couple can read one hundred books on parenting, but they can't truly know what it's like to have a kid—until they have a kid. Even then they won't be able to articulate perfectly the mystery and beauty and pain of their love.

This is Paul's idea in speaking of Christ's infinite love. We'll never truly grasp it. The good news is we don't have to completely understand it to experience and enjoy it.

*I no longer want just to hear about you, beloved
Lord, through messengers. I no longer want to hear
doctrines about you, nor to have my emotions stirred
by people speaking of you. I yearn for your presence.*

JOHN OF THE CROSS

CHOSEN BY GOD

God decided in advance to adopt us into his own family
by bringing us to himself through Jesus Christ. This is
what he wanted to do, and it gave him great pleasure.

EPHESIANS 1:5

A child languishes in a faraway orphanage. On good days his life is bleak. On bad days, it's unthinkable.

Out of the blue, a couple shows up. With eyes full of love, they announce their intention: "We want you to come be our little boy!"

It is all so illogical, wonderful, and nonsensical. Who does such a thing, and why?

No wonder the Bible writers use adoption as a picture of salvation. It's amazing that God would choose to love us. But he does. He just does.

Can you see, in Christ, the eyes of God, brimming with love?

Adoption is a greater mercy than Adam had in paradise.
THOMAS WATSON

DEEPER THAN WORDS

Never stop praying.

1 THESSALONIANS 5:17

Is this possible? Praying *all the time*?

Not if prayer always requires

- a holy setting (i.e., a chapel);
- solitude (i.e., being all alone);
- stillness and quiet;
- closed eyes;
- eloquent words;
- a heart bursting with joy and holy passion; and
- ignoring all life's other realities.

Only someone who never drives a car could possibly hope to pray like that.

On the other hand, if prayer is a continual awareness of God—a genuine sense of needing him like you need breath and developing the habit of dialoguing with him throughout the day, until you fall asleep with your thoughts on him—then the answer is a resounding yes!

Prayer is something deeper than words. It is present in the soul before it has been formulated in words. And it abides in the soul after the last words of prayer have passed over our lips.

OLE HALLESBY

OUR ALL IN ALL

*Whom have I in heaven but you? I desire you
more than anything on earth. My health may fail,
and my spirit may grow weak, but God remains
the strength of my heart; he is mine forever.*

PSALM 73:25-26

Psalm 73 is the refreshing prayer of one of Israel's great
worship leaders. Here Asaph talks honestly about a time
when he "envied the proud" (verse 3) because they had
"everything their hearts could ever wish for" (verse 7).

It took a gracious reminder from God during worship (see verse 17) to snap the foolish, bitter Asaph back
to ultimate reality: Why envy those with trivial, earthly
riches when we can enjoy the eternal blessing of the God
who is near (see verse 28), both now and forever?

*May you be blessed forever! Although
I abandoned You, You did not abandon me.*

TERESA OF AVILA

WEARING JESUS

*All who have been united with Christ in baptism
have put on Christ, like putting on new clothes.*

GALATIANS 3:27

One of the questions regularly asked of movie stars on the red carpet is "Who are you wearing?" In other words, "What designer made you look so good?"

The apostle Paul says that to be a Christian is, in a real sense, to wear Christ. Because he lives within us, his character ought to adorn our lives like a beautiful outfit.

The next time you change clothes, think about "putting on" Christ. Let your wardrobe today consist of his "tenderhearted mercy, kindness, humility, gentleness, and patience" (Colossians 3:12).

*"Putting on Christ" . . . is not one among many
jobs a Christian has to do; and it is not a sort of
special exercise for the top class. It is the whole of
Christianity. Christianity offers nothing else at all.*

C. S. LEWIS

DEPENDENCE DAY

If the Son sets you free, you are truly free.

JOHN 8:36

Americans will spend today celebrating their independence—attending patriotic assemblies, watching parades, and eating hot dogs (the unofficial national sandwich). Tonight we'll *ooh* and *ah* over lavish fireworks displays. All because we are *free.*

Political freedom is a remarkable blessing. But it pales in comparison to the freedom that Jesus brings and offers to people of every nation.

Consider the irony: it was by declaring *independence* from God that the human race became enslaved to sin and sentenced to death. It took Jesus coming and dying to make humankind's liberation possible. Now it requires *dependence* on Christ to experience that freedom.

In the midst of celebrating today, thank God for political independence, but thank him especially for spiritual freedom through spiritual dependence.

To serve God, to love God, to enjoy God,
is the sweetest freedom in the world.

THOMAS WATSON

THE REAL SEEKER

The Son of Man came to seek and save those who are lost.

LUKE 19:10

This verse is the punch line for one of the Bible's most beloved stories.

While passing through the crowded streets of Jericho, Jesus observed Zacchaeus in a tree above the crowd. Zacchaeus, a crooked and wealthy tax collector, was despised by his neighbors. As a vertically challenged social outcast, it's likely he also despised himself.

Jesus called Zacchaeus by name and told him to get down from the tree. Zacchaeus came down from his leafy perch, took Jesus to his home, and became a new man.

Some would call Zacchaeus a "seeker." The real seeker in this story is Jesus himself.

> *So long as we imagine it is we who have to look for God, we must often lose heart. But it is the other way about—He is looking for us.*
>
> SIMON TUGWELL

THE GOOD FIGHT

*Fight the good fight for the true faith. Hold tightly to
the eternal life to which God has called you, which
you have declared so well before many witnesses.*

1 TIMOTHY 6:12

A life with God is not all about lounging in green pas-
tures (see Psalm 23:2), praising God's name with dancing
(see Psalm 149:3), and being caught up into heaven (see
2 Corinthians 12:2). We have such moments, but typically the life of faith is tough.

It's a grueling race (see 1 Corinthians 9:24) that
brings a truckload of trials (see 2 Corinthians 4:8-12).
Much of the spiritual life involves fighting against sin
and battling the great enemy who wants to take us out.

You don't have to fight the whole war today. Just
advance. Team up with some fellow troops and fight the
good fight.

Outside of Christ, I cannot; in Christ, I am more than able.

WATCHMAN NEE

IN CHRIST'S NAME

You can ask for anything in my name, and I will do it, so that the Son can bring glory to the Father. Yes, ask me for anything in my name, and I will do it!

JOHN 14:13-14

"Ask," Jesus said, "in my name."

What is this? A magical formula we can tack onto our prayers to guarantee we'll get whatever we ask? No. In ancient times a person's name represented all that was true of that individual. So when Jesus spoke of praying *in his name*, he meant, "Ask for things that are consistent with my character and mission."

Given that, should we pray for an easy life or a God-honoring life? Should we maybe be praying less about us going on vacation and more about others coming to Christ?

Never will man pray as he ought unless the Master will guide both his mouth and his heart.

JOHN CALVIN

TRUTH IN ADVERTISING

I have told you all this so that you may have peace in me.
Here on earth you will have many trials and sorrows.
But take heart, because I have overcome the world.

JOHN 16:33

Often, when Christians tell others about our faith, we emphasize all the positives.

We talk, for example, about becoming a child of God, receiving forgiveness, and enjoying life in heaven one day—and we should. But it's important to let others know how Christians struggle with temptation, endure attacks from the enemy, and experience hardship here on earth.

Jesus held nothing back. He promised otherworldly peace and ultimate victory to his followers. And he didn't hide the truth that we need such assurances, because following him will be the hardest thing any of us ever do.

All these difficulties are only platforms for the
manifestation of His grace, power and love.
HUDSON TAYLOR

PROSPERITY AND SUCCESS

Study this Book of Instruction continually. Meditate on it day and night so you will be sure to obey everything written in it. Only then will you prosper and succeed in all you do.

JOSHUA 1:8

A recent online search for "how to be successful" yielded about 740 million results. If you could absorb one of those pages per second, all day, every day—and forgo sleeping altogether—it would take over twenty-three years to learn everything the world says about success.

Or you could just look again at what this one verse says: study God's Word. Meditate on it when you're not actually looking at it. Do what it says.

This may not make you a millionaire or a household name. But God promises you'll be spiritually prosperous and, in his eyes, a success.

Apply yourself wholly to the text; apply the text wholly to yourself.

JOHANN A. BENGEL

A TOUGH TASK

Let all that I am wait quietly before
God, for my hope is in him.

PSALM 62:5

"Don't just sit there—do something!" is the operating mantra for most folks. "Get busy! Fix the problem!"

But David, in a time of trouble, counseled himself differently: "Don't just do something—sit there. Wait for God's leading."

For many of us, *wait* is the foulest of all four-letter words. And quieting all the internal noise? It's like trying to corral one hundred toddlers!

Even so, today, if you've got trouble, resist the strong urge to immediately swing into action. First, place your hope in him. Then "wait quietly before God."

Waiting itself is beneficial to us: it tries faith, exercises patience, trains submission, and endears the blessing when it comes. The Lord's people have always been a waiting people.

CHARLES H. SPURGEON

TRUE WORSHIP

God is Spirit, so those who worship him
must worship in spirit and in truth.

JOHN 4:24

Few subjects prompt as much heated debate among Christians as the subject of *worship*.

Should it be private or corporate? Formal or informal? Expressive or reserved? Loud or contemplative? Liturgical or spontaneous? Is it better to stand, sit, kneel, or raise hands? On and on it goes.

Jesus gave us only two guidelines. We must worship "in spirit"—internally, from our hearts. And we must worship "in truth"—in a way that's consistent with everything that God has revealed in his Word.

In short, the worship that God seeks (see John 4:23) and that pleases him is worship from a passionate heart and a biblically informed mind. If you have that, you can stand on your head.

I never knew how to worship until I knew how to love.
HENRY WARD BEECHER

AN UNDIVIDED HEART

God blesses those whose hearts are pure, for they will see God.

MATTHEW 5:8

What does it mean to have a *pure* heart?

One meaning is "morally clean." While we know from Scripture that no human (other than Jesus) can live a sinless life (see Romans 3:23), those who trust in Jesus and believe he took the punishment for sin are eternally clean in God's sight. We receive cleansing of our hearts regularly when we confess and forsake sinful attitudes or habits that God's Spirit shows us.

A second meaning of *pure* is "single-minded" or "wholly devoted," like the word *holy*. A pure heart is an undivided heart.

Today, ask God for a clean heart that beats for one purpose only.

It is safe to tell the pure in heart that they shall see God, for only the pure in heart want to.

C. S. LEWIS

WORKING FOR CHRIST

*Work with enthusiasm, as though you were
working for the Lord rather than for people.*

EPHESIANS 6:7

How many commercials have you seen where the boss leaves the office and the workers immediately start goofing off? It's the classic example of the phrase "When the cat's away, the mice will play."

But this verse essentially says, "Don't work hard only when your supervisor is looking over your shoulder or just before your annual review. Do top-notch work every day, from the time you show up (ideally early) until the time you call it a day. Go the extra mile and be excellent in your job."

How would your work ethic change today if you saw yourself as working for Christ? If you did everything to please him?

*If our desire is to please God, pouring water, washing dishes,
cobbling shoes, and preaching the Word is all one.*

WILLIAM TYNDALE

OUT OF THE OVERFLOW OF THE HEART

*May the words of my mouth and the meditation of my heart
be pleasing to you, O LORD, my rock and my redeemer.*

PSALM 19:14

We've all done it: blurted something out in irritation, angrily given someone a piece of our minds.

Coming back later and saying "I didn't really mean it" works about as well as a judge saying "The jury will disregard those comments." People can't unhear things any more than we can unsay them.

Here's practical help. Memorize this verse. Then make it your prayer all day, every day—before that frustrating meeting with your boss, during that conference with your child's teacher, while you're disagreeing with your spouse. Ask your Rock and Redeemer for God-pleasing words that flow from a God-pleasing heart.

*For all the disorders of the tongue, the
remedy must begin at the heart.*
ROBERT LEIGHTON

LET YOUR SOUL REST

Let my soul be at rest again,
for the LORD has been good to me.

PSALM 116:7

Our souls have two basic settings: rested and restless.

How's your soul right now? Are you rested and secure in the knowledge that God has you in his strong, good hands? Or are you twitchy and restless, like a long-tailed cat in a room full of rocking chairs?

The psalmist's brush with death brings terror, trouble, and sorrow (Psalm 116:3). He responds in two ways: he calls on God to save his life. Then he calls on his soul to rest, to turn back to the one who protects and comforts.

Why not do the same today? Speak to God. Then let your soul rest in him.

As waters are purest when they are in motion, so
saints are generally holiest when in affliction.

WILLIAM SECKER

JULY 16

A TRUE VIEW

Where is another God like you, who pardons the guilt
of the remnant, overlooking the sins of his special people?
You will not stay angry with your people forever,
because you delight in showing unfailing love.

MICAH 7:18

A. W. Tozer argued that the most important fact about us is what we believe about the character of God. A twisted understanding of God results in a twisted life; a right view solves countless temporary earthly problems.

The prophet Micah viewed our Creator as a holy, generous, compassionate God who hates sin, forgives us when we go our own way, and takes pleasure in demonstrating his loyal love to us.

Is *this* the God you see and serve? If not, turn to him and find the life you were meant for.

You can see God from anywhere if your
mind is set to love and obey Him.

A. W. TOZER

TOMORROW IS OVERRATED

---

*Don't worry about tomorrow, for tomorrow will bring
its own worries. Today's trouble is enough for today.*

MATTHEW 6:34

A bunch of things happen when we fret over tomorrow,
and none of them are good. We waste precious mental energy. We forfeit peace. Maybe worst of all, every
moment we spend getting worked up about the future
is a moment in the wonderful, beautiful present that we
simply miss.

According to Jesus, the solution to worrying about
tomorrow is "don't."

That's obviously easier said than done, but Jesus'
point here is that we can trust the Lord to care for us. So
be thankful for this moment, and be faithful in it. Then
relax. The Lord is in control.

*Worry is a cycle of inefficient thoughts
whirling around a center of fear.*

CORRIE TEN BOOM

BIRDS AND BARBERSHOPS

What is the price of five sparrows—two copper coins?
Yet God does not forget a single one of them. And the very
hairs on your head are all numbered. So don't be afraid;
you are more valuable to God than a whole flock of sparrows.

LUKE 12:6-7

Approaching the hair salon, you startle a tiny bird pecking away in a planter by the door. Once you're inside, your stylist greets you while sweeping up hair from around the chair.

Here's a real-life reminder of Jesus' immortal words. If God sees and cares for birds, how much more does he watch over you? He tracks your life situation so intimately that he knows the number of your hairs—pre- and post-haircut!

You are beloved. If you're doubting that, look at your hairbrush and smile.

A firm faith in the universal providence of God
is the solution of all earthly troubles.

B. B. WARFIELD

THE POLLYANNA TRUTH

Be on guard. Stand firm in the faith.
Be courageous. Be strong.

1 CORINTHIANS 16:13

Remember Pollyanna, the syrupy sweet girl in the classic children's book and movie who tended to focus only on happy things and dismiss hard realities?

Many Christians embrace a similar mind-set in their spiritual lives. They need to mull over the sobering words in this terse verse from the apostle Paul. Malevolent forces roam the world—"be on guard." Those fierce enemies will try to knock you down—"stand firm." Things will get unsettling, even scary at times—"be courageous." There will be moments when you will want to quit—"be strong."

The Pollyanna truth we can cling to in all this? We have a Savior who empowers us to live out such commands.

Courage is contagious. When a brave man takes
a stand, the spines of others are often stiffened.

BILLY GRAHAM

PAYING IT FORWARD

All praise to God, the Father of our Lord Jesus Christ.
God is our merciful Father and the source of all
comfort. He comforts us in all our troubles so that we
can comfort others. When they are troubled, we will be
able to give them the same comfort God has given us.

2 CORINTHIANS 1:3-4

A mom discovers a delicious recipe and passes it on to her daughter. A wily veteran shares a hard-won secret with a wide-eyed rookie. Why? Because good things are meant to be shared.

This works with comfort, too. When we find the Lord's grace and goodness in our pain, we have the opportunity—and responsibility—to pay that forward.

What hurting person could benefit from your experience of suffering and loss?

Even the saddest things can become, once we have made
peace with them, a source of wisdom and strength.

FREDERICK BUECHNER

A NEW PERSPECTIVE

*Our present troubles are small and won't last
very long. Yet they produce for us a glory that
vastly outweighs them and will last forever!*

2 CORINTHIANS 4:17

Chronic difficulty can be debilitating. We wonder, *Will
I ever get relief? Is this overwhelming problem going to be
with me forever?*

Paul was a guy who struggled and suffered as much
as anyone who ever lived. Notice his shocking statement
about life's troubles: they're small and won't last very long.

What's more, Paul suggests that our God is so great
that he will, if we let him, produce major glory from our
troubles—a glory that will last forever.

When you're in it, such claims don't erase the pain—
but they do, when trusted, fill us with hope.

*Christianity empowers its people to sit in the midst
of this world's sorrows, tasting the coming joy.*

TIMOTHY KELLER

A NEW FOCUS

*We don't look at the troubles we can see now;
rather, we fix our gaze on things that cannot be
seen. For the things we see now will soon be gone,
but the things we cannot see will last forever.*

2 CORINTHIANS 4:18

In *The Diary of an Old Soul*, George MacDonald confessed, "My eyes pull my heart." By this he meant that if we gawk at earthly things, we'll become enamored with such things. But if we fix our gaze on eternal, heavenly things, our hearts will beat for the things of God.

Where's your focus? Do you stare excessively at superficial stuff? Or do you pray for the spiritual vision to see those invisible realities that will last forever?

*If I find in myself a desire which no experience in
this world can satisfy, the most probable explanation
is that I was made for another world.*

C. S. LEWIS

EULOGIES AND EPITAPHS

---

*The Holy Spirit produces this kind of fruit in
our lives: love, joy, peace, patience, kindness,
goodness, faithfulness, gentleness, and self-control.
There is no law against these things!*

GALATIANS 5:22-23

Maybe you've been to a funeral where it was obvious everyone was struggling mightily to find good things to say about the departed. Perhaps you've been to other memorial services where immense joy for a life well lived resonated more than deep sadness.

One way or another, we each will be remembered. Why not, then, leave a legacy of Christlikeness?

How do we do this? By letting God's Holy Spirit rule in us, animate us, and empower us moment by moment.

Marvel at the fruit the Spirit produces in those who follow his promptings. And know this: such lives make for grand funerals.

*When it is a question of God's almighty
Spirit, never say, "I can't."*
OSWALD CHAMBERS

FELLOWSHIP WITH CHRIST

Now, dear children, remain in fellowship with Christ so that when he returns, you will be full of courage and not shrink back from him in shame.

1 JOHN 2:28

The biblical word *fellowship* means "sharing in common; a partnership." It implies a close relationship where the parties are on the same page.

Practically speaking, this is the mind-set a Christian should have: *I want to partner with Jesus today. I want to walk closely with him, share in his life, and share his Good News with others.*

John says those believers who "remain in fellowship with Christ" are ready for his any-minute return. They won't be like the teenager who is hosting a wild party for three hundred friends when his parents decide to come home early from vacation.

Jesus Christ does not want to be our helper; He wants to be our life.

CHARLES TRUMBULL

GOING TO CHURCH

Let us not neglect our meeting together, as some people do, but encourage one another, especially now that the day of his return is drawing near.

HEBREWS 10:25

Let's talk about going to church.

First of all, *church* isn't a building or meeting. It's all the people who have placed their faith in Jesus. So we don't really "go to church" so much as we "go to where the church is gathering together."

The writer of Hebrews says gathering like this is extremely important. We shouldn't "neglect our meeting together." Why? Because, as Christians living in a hostile world, we need to encourage one another.

By studying God's Word, praying, singing, and taking Communion together, we are reminded of life's greatest truths. We leave stronger and better equipped to make an eternal difference in the world.

The Church is the one institution that exists for those outside it.
WILLIAM TYNDALE

HOLDING THINGS LOOSELY

I came naked from my mother's womb, and I will be naked
when I leave. The LORD gave me what I had, and the
LORD has taken it away. Praise the name of the LORD!

JOB 1:21

The baby is born wearing only his birthday suit. The college grad's possessions all fit into her beat-up compact car. The elderly woman dies owning 4,500-square-foot house that's overflowing with stuff. Is it that we get more and more things as we go through life? Or is it that more and more things take hold of us?

Here Job models the proper attitude toward children, money, possessions, everything in our lives: it was God's before it was ever ours, and he can reclaim it whenever he wants. When he does, it helps to have a loose grip.

Whatever I have placed in God's hands, that I still possess.

MARTIN LUTHER

NEED RESCUE?

---

*You, O LORD, are a shield around me; you are
my glory, the one who holds my head high.*

PSALM 3:3

After David's son Absalom stole the hearts of the Israelite
people, he declared himself king. Fleeing the royal palace
in disgrace, David was subjected to the taunts of his enemies (2 Samuel 15–16).

Though he must have been discouraged, David
trusted God as (a) his sure protector ("a shield around
me"); (b) the majestic one who shone brightly in his
darkness ("my glory"); and (c) the restorer of his dignity
and confidence ("the one who holds my head high").

Whatever your tough circumstances are today, realize
this: the God of David is your God too!

*The violent winds of suffering and trouble
blow us into the Lord's protective hands.*

SADHU SUNDAR SINGH

HOLY R & R

Jesus said, "Let's go off by ourselves to a quiet place
and rest awhile." He said this because there were
so many people coming and going that Jesus and
his apostles didn't even have time to eat.

MARK 6:31

Remember the Energizer Bunny—that sunglasses-wearing rabbit of marketing fame who keeps going and going? Apparently many believers have decided the bunny is the role model for the Christian life. What else can explain all the cases of burnout in the church?

Jesus offers a better way. Though he commands us to serve, he also calls us to needed holy rest and relaxation.

Do you have regular downtime? When do you go "off duty," trusting that the Lord is still watching over your life?

If we don't come apart and rest, we'll just come apart.
VANCE HAVNER

JULY 29

JUST A LITTLE MORE

Don't love money; be satisfied with what
you have. For God has said, "I will never
fail you. I will never abandon you."

HEBREWS 13:5

Someone once asked billionaire John D. Rockefeller, "How much money is enough money?" He famously replied, "Just a little bit more."

What a snapshot of human nature! It's a rare soul who says, "I have enough"—and who enjoys sweet contentment.

No wonder this verse condemns the love of money and counsels, "Be satisfied with what you have." Consider all the people who have put their hopes in this investment or that—only to become victims of Ponzi schemes or massive market dips.

How much better to love the one who will never let us down and to say of *him*, "Just a little bit more."

If your desires be endless, your cares and fears will be so too.
THOMAS FULLER

WHEN BEING BROKEN IS GOOD

The sacrifice you desire is a broken spirit. You will not reject a broken and repentant heart, O God.

PSALM 51:17

Some try to ignore guilt through busyness and distraction. Some attempt to drown it with various substances. Others try escaping by walling themselves off emotionally or even moving away and trying to start over. Still others make sacrifices to compensate for their wrong. They give money to charity, or they punish themselves in some way.

David shows us the best way to deal with guilt: confess it. Just come clean. When we humbly admit our sin—and our inability to fix ourselves—God forgives and restores.

Remember, only the broken get to be made whole.

The prayer that prevails is not the works of lips and fingertips. It is the cry of a broken heart and the travail of a stricken soul.

SAMUEL CHADWICK

THE SULKING PROPHET

You are a merciful and compassionate God,
slow to get angry and filled with unfailing love.

JONAH 4:2

When God told Jonah to go and urge the people of Nineveh to repent, he answered no. After a little convincing (involving a giant fish) Jonah reluctantly complied. When the people turned to God, the prophet sulked.

Jonah's story is a window into God's heart. He wants all people everywhere to experience forgiveness, not judgment. This story warns us as believers to keep our hearts from becoming hard toward those who are far from God.

Where is God calling you to go today?

Any method of evangelism will work—if God is in it.
LEONARD RAVENHILL

REFUSING BLESSING?

This is what the Sovereign LORD, the Holy One of Israel, says: "Only in returning to me and resting in me will you be saved. In quietness and confidence is your strength. But you would have none of it."

ISAIAH 30:15

The more hard-hearted God's people became, the more God sent prophets like Isaiah. Their messages, oracles, and visions were a mixed bag of rebukes and reassurances. They vividly communicated both God's holiness and his loyal love.

In this beloved verse, we see God tenderly pleading with his wayward people. By "returning" (literally "repenting") and resting in God they could have experienced deliverance. This was God's heart for them. But note their response: they "would have none of it."

How are you responding to God's love for you? Will you return to him today?

Therefore let us repent and pass from ignorance to knowledge, from foolishness to wisdom, from licentiousness to self-control, from injustice to righteousness, from godlessness to God.

CLEMENT OF ALEXANDRIA

SOVEREIGNTY 101

Joseph replied, . . . "You intended to harm me,
but God intended it all for good. He brought me to this
position so I could save the lives of many people."

GENESIS 50:20

The details of the story of Joseph, Jacob's golden child, never get old.

Joseph was sold into slavery by his bitter brothers. He was falsely accused of sexual assault by his Egyptian masters and thrown into prison. From prison, Joseph was unexpectedly promoted to the office of prime minister. While he was prime minister, he was reunited with his brothers through head-shaking circumstances and became the human "savior" of both his family and the nation of Egypt.

What a powerful reminder that God controls all things. He thwarts the sinful actions of human beings. He works *in* and *through* seemingly random events to accomplish his purposes. He is *always* orchestrating.

Trust these truths today—especially if you're in a mess. See your pain as a prelude to something glorious and good.

Many men owe the grandeur of their lives
to their tremendous difficulties.

CHARLES H. SPURGEON

LETTING GO

If you try to hang on to your life, you will lose it.
But if you give up your life for my sake and for
the sake of the Good News, you will save it.

MARK 8:35

Saving one's life often calls for counterintuitive measures. Drowning? *Relax.* Being attacked by a mama grizzly? *Don't run—fall down and play dead.*

Jesus said it's the same in life. If we go through this world feverishly clutching at stuff and pridefully thinking we can save ourselves, we'll lose it all. But if we let go of all else and follow the Lord by faith, we'll gain, in the end, everything that's worth having.

If letting go seems to you like a death sentence, remember you're following the one who leads you *through* death to life.

Faith talks in the language of God.
Doubt talks in the language of man.

E. W. KENYON

PRAYING LIKE JESUS

Jesus often withdrew to the wilderness for prayer.

LUKE 5:16

Jesus spent his life devoted to serving his heavenly Father. His goal was to *please* the Father (John 8:29) by doing his will (John 4:34). His mission was to *reveal* the Father (Luke 10:22; John 1:18). And, as this verse shows, Jesus' desire was to slip away, whenever possible, from the craziness of life in order to *spend time with* his Father in prayer.

For Jesus, prayer wasn't an obligatory exercise or religious ritual. It was desirable and necessary alone time with the Father.

What's prayer like for you—more duty or delight? If it's the former, ask God to make it the latter!

Oh, if only I could pray the way this dog watches the meat! All his thoughts are concentrated on the piece of meat. Otherwise he has no thought, wish, or hope.

MARTIN LUTHER

AN OFFER WE CAN'T REFUSE

I will make you into a great nation. I will bless you and make you famous, and you will be a blessing to others.

GENESIS 12:2

Out of the blue, God barged into Abraham's life and told him to start packing. He announced that Abraham and his wife, who were advanced in years and childless, would become the parents of a great nation. He promised land, fame, and many descendants—and vowed to bless the whole world through Abraham.

Surely Abraham's mind was spinning, his mouth hanging open. These outlandish promises came with zero details. But Abraham took the Almighty at his word and took off. His life—and the fate of the world—was forever changed in that moment.

What's God calling *you* to do in this moment?

Why don't you turn your life over to Christ? He can do more with it than you can.

D. L. MOODY

OUR CALLING CARD

Dear friends, let us continue to love one another,
for love comes from God. Anyone who loves is a
child of God and knows God. But anyone who does
not love does not know God, for God is love.

1 JOHN 4:7-8

What identifies a follower of Jesus? Spouting the right beliefs? Attending church regularly? Wearing "Christian" T-shirts?

Nothing's wrong with those things. But none of them are *proof* that a person is a child of God. According to John, the one thing that shows we know God is showing our love for others.

Loving people doesn't always come easily for us. However, the twin bits of good news here are that "God *is* love" and "love comes from God." This means when we struggle to love someone God can enable us to do it!

Do not waste time bothering whether you
"love" your neighbour; act as if you did.

C. S. LEWIS

GOD OF ANTHILLS

What are mere mortals that you should think about them, human beings that you should care for them?

PSALM 8:4

Would you think it weird if the world's richest man became emotionally attached to an anthill in his front lawn? What if he stood there twenty-four hours a day for seven days a week, watching over his beloved little insects? What if he left his estate to them?

In Psalm 8, David marvels at the mystery of God Almighty caring for us and crowning us with glory and honor. Why would a majestic creator make such a big deal of pitiful creatures like us?

It's impossible to fathom. But there's no missing this truth: you are special to God, and he is wild about you. He made you for much more than you think.

Bring me a worm that can comprehend a man, and then I will show you a man that can comprehend the triune God.

JOHN WESLEY

PAUSE AND RECHARGE

*I gave them my Sabbath days of rest as a sign between
them and me. It was to remind them that I am
the LORD, who had set them apart to be holy.*

EZEKIEL 20:12

The Hebrew words *Sabbath* and *rested* come from the
same root word that means "pause," "stop," or "cease."

The Sabbath day, then, is a day earmarked by God
for the cessation of all regular duties. It's the Lord's way
of saying, "Take a break. Get some rest. Go off duty and
trust that I'm still 'on.'"

But it's more than physical *rest*. The people of God
also recharge spiritually and emotionally through *remembrance* and *rejoicing*. During this weekly break from all
the hustle and bustle of life, the goal is to recount God's
faithfulness and give thanks for his goodness.

As fewer and fewer people observe the Sabbath, more
and more people experience burnout. There might be a
connection.

*If we refuse rest until we are finished,
we will never rest until we die.*

WAYNE MULLER

"YOU REMIND ME OF YOUR FATHER"

*God blesses those who work for peace, for they
will be called the children of God.*

MATTHEW 5:9

We typically think of God as our Creator, Savior, Judge, and Father. But how often do we think of him as our Peacemaker?

When we became God's enemies by sinning (see Romans 5:10), God pursued peace with us. He "was in Christ, reconciling the world to himself" (2 Corinthians 5:19).

No wonder God has a special affection for those who engage in the difficult process of trying to help people find peace with God and with one other. When we are peacemakers, we resemble our Father in heaven.

In what relationship today do you need to work for peace?

*The followers of Jesus have been called to peace. When he
called them they found their peace, for he is their peace.*

DIETRICH BONHOEFFER

LIFE BEYOND MEASURE

The thief's purpose is to steal and kill and destroy. My
purpose is to give them a rich and satisfying life.

JOHN 10:10

There's a reason fairy tales often end with the words "and they lived happily ever after"—people want to be happy!

Thankfully, God wants that for us too. We can say this with absolute confidence because of Jesus' stated purpose of wanting to give people a rich and satisfying life.

"Rich and satisfying" is the translation of a single Greek word that means "beyond measure, extraordinary, excessive." The word connotes a life that is advantageous, exceptional, more than expected, and beyond the norm.

Sound good to you? You can have it. However, you won't find such life anywhere but in the Lord, the "one who is life itself" (1 John 1:2).

While all men seek after happiness, scarcely
one in a hundred looks for it from God.

JOHN CALVIN

THE PROBLEM WITH "MY" AND "MINE"

The earth is the LORD's, and everything in it.
The world and all its people belong to him.

PSALM 24:1

Take this self-test:

1. My most cherished possession is _____.
2. On a 1–10 scale (1 means "I'd yawn" and 10 means "I might *never* recover!"), I'd be a _____ if I lost that item.
3. Something I'd have a hard time loaning out is _____.

This verse is an important reminder. It tells us that God owns *everything*. Our lives, families, assets, possessions, and futures *all* belong to him.

We're mere managers of all that God has entrusted to our care. So when he asks for something, it's best not to clutch it too tightly.

In the total expanse of human life there is not a
single square inch of which the Christ, who alone
is sovereign, does not declare, "That is mine!"

ABRAHAM KUYPER

ETERNAL LIFE *NOW*

*This is the way to have eternal life—to know you, the only
true God, and Jesus Christ, the one you sent to earth.*

JOHN 17:3

People have many different ideas of how to describe *eternal
life*. Some think it's a divine promise that becomes good
the moment you die. Others would describe it as a forever
extension of this life (only with *serious* upgrades). Most
people use it as a synonym for *heaven*.

But notice how Jesus described it in the verse for today.
It's not an abstract substance; it's a *relationship with God
through Jesus*. This means we enter eternal life the moment
we trust in Jesus. We don't have to wait for heaven to get
this life. Jesus brings it to us here and now.

The more you get to know God, the more richly you
will experience this new, true life.

*The soul's deepest thirst is for God himself, who has made
us so that we can never be satisfied without him.*

F. F. BRUCE

PRAYING FOR US

*I am praying not only for these disciples but also for all
who will ever believe in me through their message.*

JOHN 17:20

Hearing a friend say "I am praying for you" is one of life's sweeter blessings. Knowing that someone cares about you and willingly brings up what you're going through in their conversations with God surely encourages your heart.

So how does your heart respond when you read this verse about the *Son of God* praying specifically for *you*? If you're a believer, Jesus prayed for you the night before he went to the cross.

When you couple this verse with others that show Jesus is, even now, interceding for us before the throne of God (see Romans 8:34; Hebrews 7:25), it's hard not to feel reenergized.

*No man can do me a truer kindness in
this world than to pray for me.*

CHARLES H. SPURGEON

TRIFLING WITH GOD?

*The LORD is slow to get angry, but his power is
great, and he never lets the guilty go unpunished.
He displays his power in the whirlwind and the storm.
The billowing clouds are the dust beneath his feet.*

NAHUM 1:3

Pulitzer Prize–winning author Annie Dillard once wrote
an essay about the mindless way people approach worship. "Does anyone have the foggiest idea what sort of
power we so blithely invoke? . . . We should all be wearing
crash helmets."

Those words sound like Nahum's stern message to
the godless Assyrians. God is not to be trifled with. "The
LORD is good . . . close to those who trust in him. But he
will sweep away his enemies" (Nahum 1:7-8).

We would do well to always remember that God is
God—he's not a Sunday morning program or a help hot-
line; he's the almighty Creator of the universe.

*Those who will not deliver themselves into the hand of God's
mercy cannot be delivered out of the hand of his justice.*

MATTHEW HENRY

ASK AWAY

Keep on asking, and you will receive what you ask for. Keep on seeking, and you will find. Keep on knocking, and the door will be opened to you.

MATTHEW 7:7

The child who keeps begging you to play, the woodpecker that won't stop hammering at the tree outside your window—they're reminding you of a great truth.

It's the same lesson Jesus taught about prayer in his famous Sermon on the Mount: Be persistent! Don't give up! God rewards relentlessness.

On another occasion, Jesus told a story about a widow who kept pestering a judge until he ruled in her favor (Luke 18:1-8). It makes you wonder how many blessings we miss out on because we quit too soon.

Some people think God does not like to be troubled with our constant coming and asking. The only way to trouble God is not to come at all.

D. L. MOODY

AWARDS DAY

We must all stand before Christ to be judged. We will each receive whatever we deserve for the good or evil we have done in this earthly body.

2 CORINTHIANS 5:10

Have you ever nervously waited to hear your name called—perhaps with the results of a tryout or news about a special award?

This famous verse says that every follower of Jesus will one day have a face-to-face appointment with Jesus. The purpose of this meeting is not to determine *where* we will go (for Christians, that matter has already been decided) but rather *how* we served Christ in this life.

Rather than fearing this upcoming reality, let it motivate you to faithfully serve the Lord. Ask Jesus to empower you to live this day with one eye on that day.

Let us remember, there is One who daily records all we do for Him, and sees more beauty in His servants' work than His servants do themselves.

J. C. RYLE

A PROMISE FOR YOU?

*"I know the plans I have for you," says the
LORD. "They are plans for good and not for
disaster, to give you a future and a hope."*

JEREMIAH 29:11

Some Christians are quick to remind fellow believers
when they quote this verse: "That's a promise explicitly
for the *people of Israel* who were headed for exile—that
God would restore *Israel* one day."

Absolutely true. God was telling his ancient people,
"Despite your sin, I'm not done with you."

The faithfulness that God shows Israel continues
today in his relationship with the church. God has promised all Christians an exciting, hope-filled future (see
1 John 3:2). We are assured that God works everything
"together for the good of those who love God" (Romans
8:28).

The details of God's promises do differ, but the good
heart of the Promiser is unchanging.

God never made a promise that was too good to be true.

D. L. MOODY

SYMBOL OF GRACE

God said, "I am giving you a sign of my covenant with you and with all living creatures, for all generations to come. I have placed my rainbow in the clouds. It is the sign of my covenant with you and with all the earth."

GENESIS 9:12-13

The world was in dire condition. It was so bad that God started over with just one family: Noah's.

Noah was not a perfect man, but he was faithful (see Hebrews 11:7). And through Noah, God extended grace to humankind. He gave us a second chance.

God seems to be in the business of second chances. He doesn't give up on us easily. Next time you see a rainbow in the sky, you can remember his promise to never flood the earth again, and you can also remember his promise to keep you as his child. Forever.

Grace, like water, always flows downward, to the lowest place.

PHILIP YANCEY

SINNERS WANTED

*Jesus . . . told them, "Healthy people don't need a doctor—
sick people do. I have come to call not those who think they
are righteous, but those who know they are sinners."*

MARK 2:17

The gospel is for sinners—for admittedly rebellious, broken people.

It's for hookers and hypocrites, for cheaters, abusers, and overeaters. It's for serial killers and compulsive liars. It's for those addicted to porn or meth or shopping or people-pleasing.

Are you a racist, a gossip, a self-righteous judge of others? Are you consumed by greed or pride, envy or bitterness, hatred or unforgiveness? If so, the gospel is for you.

The gospel of Jesus provides forgiveness and healing for all who want it. But it does nothing for people who don't believe they need it.

*God creates out of nothing. Therefore, until a man
is nothing, God can make nothing out of him.*

MARTIN LUTHER

HELP FROM ABOVE

I look up to the mountains—does my help come from there?
My help comes from the LORD, who made heaven and earth!

PSALM 121:1-2

The Israelites sang these words as they made their way up Mount Zion to Jerusalem for holidays celebrated at the Temple. The words reminded the people of God to look up to the one who watches over them.

Four times in this short song, the psalmist describes God as the "watcher" of Israel. The Hebrew word *shamar* means "keeper, guard, protector."

This is who our God is. Today if you have troubles all around you, look above you. Your help comes from the Lord.

Let your cares drive you to God. I shall not mind if you have
many of them if each one leads you to prayer. If every fret
makes you lean more on the Beloved, it will be a benefit.

CHARLES H. SPURGEON

FILLED TO OVERFLOWING

---

*I pray that God, the source of hope, will fill you
completely with joy and peace because you trust
in him. Then you will overflow with confident
hope through the power of the Holy Spirit.*

ROMANS 15:13

If you've ever had a bout with burnout or experienced a season of spiritual dryness, then you know what it's like to be *empty*—nothing in the old tank, no drive, no motivation, no oomph. If you feel much of anything, it's just blah, flat indifference. You wonder if you'll ever feel alive again.

If you're feeling emotionally and spiritually numb, this prayer of the apostle Paul is perfect for you, too.

Ask God's Spirit to infuse you with the confident, joyful expectation of better days.

*Before we pray that God would fill us, I believe we
ought to pray that He would empty us. There must
be an emptying before there can be a filling.*

D. L. MOODY

LIFE AFTER DEATH

Jesus told her, "I am the resurrection and the life. Anyone who believes in me will live, even after dying."

JOHN 11:25

Try to wrap your mind around this scene. Standing outside a tomb, surrounded by mourners, Jesus declared that he is life itself—and more powerful than death.

Jesus' words must have seemed to witnesses like nothing more than crazy talk, except that he then proceeded to call his embalmed friend Lazarus (certifiably dead for *four days*) out of his tomb—giving credence to Jesus' claims.

In this mind-boggling miracle, and by his own resurrection not long after, Jesus was giving us a preview of what's to come. Death isn't the last word for believers. *Life* is.

We will not be disembodied spirits in the world to come, but redeemed spirits, in redeemed bodies, in a redeemed universe.

R. A. TORREY

NO FAVORITES

*Peter replied, "I see very clearly that
God shows no favoritism."*

ACTS 10:34

Favoritism is routine in a fallen world. If you have money, power, or beauty, you can get preferred treatment. If you have connections, you can pull strings and gain an unfair advantage over regular people. Most in "the favorite club" become insufferable.

As God's chosen people, the people of Israel developed an elitist mind-set and looked down their noses at Gentiles.

It took a couple of divine visions for Peter to realize that God loves the whole world (and not just those with a Jewish heritage). He learned what we all need to take to heart: in God's Kingdom, no one is more important than another. God calls us to different lives and tasks, but he loves us just the same.

*If we approach each person we meet as an opportunity
to demonstrate love, we'll make good progress at
putting away prejudice from our midst.*

CHARLES R. SWINDOLL

THE SCHOOL OF PRAYER

Once Jesus was in a certain place praying. As he finished,
one of his disciples came to him and said, "Lord,
teach us to pray, just as John taught his disciples."

LUKE 11:1

People approach prayer in many different ways. When it comes to prayer, it's not uncommon for us to

- be indifferent about it,
- wonder about it,
- discuss it,
- debate whether it really makes a difference,
- watch others do it,
- do a Bible study on the subject, and
- read books about it.

The disciple in this well-loved verse shows us that we can simply ask Jesus to teach us how to pray—which, if you think about it, is a prayer that gets answered in the very praying of it.

The main lesson about prayer is just this: Do it! Do it!
Do it! You want to be taught to pray. My answer is
pray and never faint, and then you shall never fail.

JOHN LAIDLAW

TURNING TO GOD

God overlooked people's ignorance about these things
in earlier times, but now he commands everyone
everywhere to repent of their sins and turn to him.

ACTS 17:30

Yesterday, Bill's doctor told him to change his diet, lose some weight, and start exercising—or risk becoming diabetic. Today, Becky started driving one direction, but the map app on her smartphone told her to turn around and go down a different highway. Correction, though sometimes humbling, is a good thing, right?

So why do we bristle when the Word of God, the Spirit of God, or the people of God urge us to alter our course?

Repentance is seeing what's true and then adjusting. It's choosing right over wrong, light over darkness, security over danger. Repentance is just plain smart. Be a willing repenter today.

Repentance . . . is the grace of a lifetime, like faith itself. . . .
Repentance is the inseparable companion of faith.

CHARLES H. SPURGEON

BE A GOOD WORKER

Work hard so you can present yourself to God and receive his approval. Be a good worker, one who does not need to be ashamed and who correctly explains the word of truth.

2 TIMOTHY 2:15

Sometimes, understanding the Bible can seem daunting. How do we figure out the hard parts? How will we answer the critics? How will we help the seekers?

This verse grounds us in what really matters: work hard to please God; and work hard to understand his Word so that you can explain it to others—simply and straightforwardly.

We don't have to be gifted communicators to share God's Word. But we do have to study it so that when the opportunity arises, the Holy Spirit can help us share what we already know.

I never saw a fruit-bearing Christian who was not a student of the Bible.

D. L. MOODY

I AM

God replied to Moses, "I AM WHO I AM. Say this to the people of Israel: I AM has sent me to you."

EXODUS 3:14

Moses was tending sheep when out of the blue—or more precisely, out of a burning bush—God said, "You must lead my people Israel out of Egypt" (Exodus 3:10).

After a brief protest, Moses essentially asked, "Who are you?" God replied, "I AM WHO I AM."

This cryptic name (derived from the Hebrew verb *hayah*, which means "to be" or "to exist") identifies God as the eternal, uncaused, and self-sufficient one. He doesn't depend on anyone or anything; rather, he's the one on whom *everyone and everything* can depend.

Pretty good encouragement for anyone facing a giant task.

Wherever Jesus may lead us, He goes before us. If we don't know where we go, at least we know with whom we go.

CHARLES H. SPURGEON

THE GOLDEN RULE

Do to others as you would like them to do to you.

LUKE 6:31

Many of the world's religions have a version of the Golden Rule. And why not? Even a young child can understand that if everyone obeyed this one simple precept, the world would be a safer, kinder place. Even irreligious people can get on board because it says nothing about God or faith.

But when Jesus said this, he wasn't talking about baking a pie for a sweet neighbor. Rather, he wants us to show kindness to those who curse us and to pray for our enemies. If we're honest, no one consistently lives like this.

The thrust of Jesus' gospel is that ideas like the Golden Rule are only possible when Jesus lives in us. More than his rules, we need him ruling in our hearts.

For understanding in spiritual matters, the golden rule is not intellect but obedience.

OSWALD CHAMBERS

SEEING THE INFINITE

---

*No one has ever seen God. But the unique
One, who is himself God, is near to the Father's
heart. He has revealed God to us.*

JOHN 1:18

Since his essential nature is Spirit (see John 4:24), God is invisible (see Colossians 1:15). "No human eye has ever seen him, nor ever will" (1 Timothy 6:16).

Skeptics smirk, "How convenient! I guess that makes God sort of like the tooth fairy."

Uh, no. In Jesus, God "became human and made his home among us" (John 1:14). Christ came not only to save us but also to *reveal* (alternatively, "to introduce, present, explain") God to humankind.

We can't see God, but had you lived in Nazareth in, say, AD 19, you could have seen—even shaken hands with—the unique God-man.

*[Jesus] was GOD and man in one person, that GOD
and man might be happy together again.*
GEORGE WHITEFIELD

LIKE JESUS

*God knew his people in advance, and he chose them
to become like his Son, so that his Son would be the
firstborn among many brothers and sisters.*

ROMANS 8:29

Remember the prevailing question from your childhood:
"What do you want to be when you grow up?" Perhaps
people still ask you this sometimes.

Here's the best answer to that question: "Like Jesus."

This is God's plan! He is making believers like his
Son. He wants to see Christ "fully developed in your
lives" (Galatians 4:19).

Some days we don't see much transformation taking
place. But keep letting God's Word permeate your heart
and mind. Cooperate with the nudging of the Spirit,
then watch.

*We are, not metaphorically but in very truth, a
Divine work of art, something that God is making,
and therefore something with which He will not
be satisfied until it has a certain character.*

C. S. LEWIS

KILLING SIN

Put to death the sinful, earthly things lurking within you.
Have nothing to do with sexual immorality, impurity,
lust, and evil desires. Don't be greedy, for a greedy person
is an idolater, worshiping the things of this world.

COLOSSIANS 3:5

"You must not murder," the Bible explicitly commands
(Exodus 20:13).

There's one exception to that command. Here
Christians are called to put to death the evil desires that
lurk in our hearts and pop up in our lives.

In truth, we've already been "crucified with Christ"
(Galatians 2:20), meaning we must continually consider
our old nature dead and buried. When wrong desires
come, we don't invite them in and indulge them. Instead,
we treat them with holy violence: we kill them.

If Christ has died for me, ungodly as I am,
. . . I cannot trifle with the evil that slew my best Friend.

CHARLES H. SPURGEON

NEW AND IMPROVED

---

*This means that anyone who belongs to Christ has become
a new person. The old life is gone; a new life has begun!*

2 CORINTHIANS 5:17

Why do marketers love the phrase *new and improved*?
Because consumers are suckers for upgrades. Smartphones,
laundry detergent, cookies—it doesn't matter. For us, *new
and improved* beats *old and dying* any day of the week.

If, however, we want complete renewal, the kind of
newness that never fades, we have to look up. When we
trust Jesus to forgive us and live in us, we get a new standing with God, a new identity, new purpose, new power,
new desires—in short, a whole new life.

The life of faith then becomes all about learning how
to live from our new hearts.

*Forgiveness, cleansing, regeneration, the Holy
Spirit, all answers to prayer are given to faith and
received by faith. There is no other way.*

A. W. TOZER

SEEING GOD SING

The LORD your God is living among you. He is
a mighty savior. He will take delight in you with
gladness. With his love, he will calm all your fears.
He will rejoice over you with joyful songs.

ZEPHANIAH 3:17

Many Christians don't typically think of God as "happy."
They think the King of the universe must be all business,
all the time—with a furrowed brow, a grim look as he
addresses all the troubles in this world.

Then we read a verse like this. God delighted? Glad?
Rejoicing over his people with joyful songs?

Ponder that description today. How does this picture
alter your view of the Lord? How does it change the way
you view yourself?

What if God were frustrated and despondent and
gloomy and dismal and discontented and dejected?
Could we join David and say, "O God, you are my
God . . . my soul thirsts for . . . ? I don't think so.

JOHN PIPER

SPEAK LIFE

*Don't use foul or abusive language. Let everything
you say be good and helpful, so that your words will
be an encouragement to those who hear them.*

EPHESIANS 4:29

"Think before you speak." Sounds like such simple advice,
right? But it can be so hard for so many. Sometimes our
tongues are like wild horses, constantly bucking off
authority and trying to run away.

Thank God for the Holy Spirit, who can help us control our tongues, one word at a time. In Proverbs 18:21,
King Solomon tells us that our tongues have the power
of life and death. If we focus on honoring God with our
language, we can choose to speak life every time. But we
have to make a conscious effort, *every time.*

*What power words can hold! Properly presented, they can
paint an absolutely credible picture of a person's heart.*

GARY SMALLEY

MAKING PROGRESS IN THE DARK

Your word is a lamp to guide my feet and a light for my path.

PSALM 119:105

Novelist E. L. Doctorow once compared writing books to "driving at night in the fog. You can only see as far as your headlights, but you can make the whole trip that way."

That's actually a good description of living by faith. In the spiritual life, we encounter long, dark stretches where the way forward is sketchy, even scary.

Thank God for his Word! While the Bible doesn't reveal the details of your life next week or next year, it always provides enough light for you to take the next few steps.

If you're on a dimly lit path these days, take heart. God's "flashlight of truth," plus a little bit of faith, will help you see all the way home.

Half our fears arise from neglect of the Bible.
CHARLES H. SPURGEON

SHINE!

You are the light of the world—like a city
on a hilltop that cannot be hidden.

MATTHEW 5:14

Picture people who are blindfolded stumbling around in the dark.

It's hard to think of a more hopeless, helpless image. But that's the biblical description of sinful people separated from God (see 2 Corinthians 4:4). Apart from God's grace, we *can't* see—and don't even *want* to see— God's truth (see John 3:19).

Thankfully, Jesus, "the light of the world" (John 8:12), came to turn on the lights in our dark hearts (see John 12:46). When he opens our eyes and takes up residence within us, we become "people of light" (Ephesians 5:8).

Today God wants the light of Jesus to "shine in our hearts" (2 Corinthians 4:6) and penetrate the world's darkness. Some will be drawn to that light. Others will flee. Shine anyway!

All the darkness in the world cannot
extinguish the light of a single candle.
ATTRIBUTED TO FRANCIS OF ASSISI

LOYAL LOVE

Don't ask me to leave you and turn back. Wherever you go, I will go; wherever you live, I will live. Your people will be my people, and your God will be my God.

RUTH 1:16

Would it disappoint you to learn this great statement of devotion (repeated so often at weddings) was spoken not by some starry-eyed lovebird but by *a young widow to her mother-in-law*?

It's true. When Naomi decided to leave Moab and return to her native Israel, Ruth grabbed her suitcase and followed her mother-in-law out the door. When Naomi protested, Ruth uttered these famous words.

Though this verse doesn't describe romantic love, Ruth's commitment to Naomi is still beautiful. Because of her faithfulness, Ruth eventually remarried and became the great-grandmother of King David—and an ancestor of the King of kings.

Nothing shapes your life more than the commitments you choose to make.

RICK WARREN

BEING SAVED

*The message of the cross is foolish to those who
are headed for destruction! But we who are being
saved know it is the very power of God.*

1 CORINTHIANS 1:18

The message of the cross *does* seem foolish: Jesus died so that we could find life. At his weakest, Christ was strongest.

God, in love, stepped out of eternity into history in the person of Jesus. After living a flawless life, he allowed sinful men to hammer him to a cross.

The one who is life itself laid down his life, and by his sacrifice, cosmic justice was served. The sin of humankind was paid for. Full forgiveness is now available. New life is possible.

What's the catch? There is none. When we stop playing God and start trusting Jesus, we are saved.

That may sound crazy. But it's true.

*To believe on the Lord Jesus Christ is
simply to take Him at His word.*

D. L. MOODY

GOD'S BIG HANDS

Don't be afraid, for I am with you. Don't be discouraged,
for I am your God. I will strengthen you and help you.
I will hold you up with my victorious right hand.

ISAIAH 41:10

In this familiar passage, we see the heart of our God.
Look at what he offers his scared and discouraged people:

"I am with you": I haven't gone anywhere, even when
it seems that way. You have my constant *presence*.

"I will strengthen you": Remember, though you get
tired, I don't. You have my limitless *power*.

"I will hold you up": You're not going to slip or fall or
drown. I've got you. You have my sure *protection*.

As you think about your life, which of these truths
means the most to you today?

There is more safety with Christ in the tempest,
then without Christ in the calme waters.

ALEXANDER GROSSE

HE IS LORD

*Jesus came and told his disciples, "I have been
given all authority in heaven and on earth."*

MATTHEW 28:18

From the time we're born until the day we die, we are
subjected to a parade of authority figures: parents, teachers, coaches, professors, bosses, governing officials and
councils, law enforcement personnel, judges, tax officials,
licensing agencies.

And who's the authority over all these authorities?
According to Jesus, he is!

This pronouncement—the "preamble" of the great
commission—is breathtaking. Christ claims all authority in heaven and on earth. He's saying he's Lord, Master,
Ruler, King of the *universe*.

Given that, shouldn't we acknowledge his authority
in our hearts and lives?

*Of all the titles of Jesus the title Lord became by far the
most commonly used, widespread, and theologically
important. It would hardly be going too far to say that
the word Lord became a synonym for the name of Jesus.*

WILLIAM BARCLAY

MARCHING ORDERS

*Go and make disciples of all the nations, baptizing them in
the name of the Father and the Son and the Holy Spirit.*

MATTHEW 28:19

Jesus began his ministry by inviting a few average guys to
come and *be* his disciples.

He concluded his earthly ministry by commanding
these trained followers to go and make other disciples,
all over the world.

In other words, Jesus was saying, "Repeat the process.
Take the Good News everywhere. As people respond in
faith, baptize them. Then show them how to live out the
gospel. Help them learn and grow. Show them how to
minister. When the time is right, launch them to repeat
the process. Don't stop till I return."

Two questions: Who is helping you follow Jesus?
Whom are you helping?

The gospel is only good news if it gets there in time.
CARL F. H. HENRY

PASSING IT ON

---

*Teach these new disciples to obey all the commands
I have given you. And be sure of this: I am with
you always, even to the end of the age.*

MATTHEW 28:20

A master plumber hires a high school student and teaches him about sewer lines and septic tanks. Everything he knows about fixing pipes, installing toilets, and unclogging drains he explains and demonstrates for the boy. After a few years the boy becomes a master plumber himself.

This is discipleship. The word *disciple* simply means "student or learner." Older, wiser mentors share, verbally and by example, all the lessons and skills they've acquired with those who are eager to learn.

Being a disciple of Jesus means knowing him and his teachings and sharing what you discover with another.

Are you learning and then passing on all you've learned?

The best learning I had came from teaching.

CORRIE TEN BOOM

LIVING SANCTUARIES

I love your sanctuary, LORD, the place
where your glorious presence dwells.

PSALM 26:8

The word *sanctuary* means "holy or sacred place." In Moses' day, the Tabernacle was Israel's sanctuary. By the time of Solomon, this portable tent was replaced by a permanent Temple in Jerusalem.

The sanctuary was where the people of Israel worshiped and the place where God was believed to dwell. Occasionally God's presence would fill the sanctuary with smoke and fire!

After Christ's life, death, resurrection, and ascension, and the coming of the Spirit at Pentecost (Acts 2), believers—both individually (1 Corinthians 6:19) and collectively (1 Corinthians 3:16-17)—became God's sanctuary.

This means there aren't any more "holy places" in the same sense as the Temple, but lots of holy people—living sanctuaries where all people everywhere can encounter God.

The Christian does not go to the temple to worship.
The Christian takes the temple with him or her.

RAVI ZACHARIAS

PERFECT PARENT

*If you sinful people know how to give good gifts to
your children, how much more will your heavenly
Father give good gifts to those who ask him.*

MATTHEW 7:11

Vince and Kimberly have two precious little girls. Their
girls are in foster care because Vince and Kimberly are in
frequent trouble with the law.

Here's what's interesting: during supervised visits
with their girls, Vince and Kimberly come alive. Their
eyes dance. They bring presents and talk lovingly about
their dreams for their girls.

The whole situation is dysfunctional and heart-
breaking, but it's a powerful reminder: if badly broken
parents desperately want to give their kids every good
thing, how much more must our perfect heavenly Father
want only the best for us?

Implant in our hearts a comforting trust in your fatherly love.
MARTIN LUTHER

TOO HARD?

*I am the LORD, the God of all the peoples of
the world. Is anything too hard for me?*

JEREMIAH 32:27

Jeremiah's hopeless dilemma was watching the fearsome Babylonian army surround Jerusalem and wondering how God was going to make good on his promises to his people.

Your "impossible" situation surely looks different: perhaps you're dealing with the death of a spouse or child, or facing the trauma of a divorce. Maybe you've failed to find a decent job in a tough economy. It's possible that you're lamenting your inability to fix a horribly broken relationship, or you're trying to overcome an addiction.

God answered the prophet's questions with an even better question: "Is anything too hard for me?" Whenever you're tempted to give in to despair, hear the Almighty whispering those words to you.

*He has at His command all the power in the
universe. . . . All His acts are done without effort.*

A. W. TOZER

BRINGING US HOME

*Christ suffered for our sins once for all time.
He never sinned, but he died for sinners to bring
you safely home to God. He suffered physical
death, but he was raised to life in the Spirit.*

1 PETER 3:18

The old patriarch dies on a Tuesday. By Friday evening the entire extended family has gathered from all over to celebrate his life.

Say what you will about death, it does at least one thing well: it brings people home.

The ultimate example of this, of course, is the gospel. We were sinful and lost, alienated from God and one another. But praise God for Jesus Christ! His death for sinners (and resurrection to life in the Spirit) is what brings us safely home to God.

*Come home, come home, ye who are weary,
come home; earnestly, tenderly, Jesus is
calling, calling, O sinner, come home!*

WILL L. THOMPSON

D-O-N-E

*He saved us, not because of the righteous things we had
done, but because of his mercy. He washed away our sins,
giving us a new birth and new life through the Holy Spirit.*

TITUS 3:5

Some people think that religion is spelled D-O. It's all
the things people do to win God's favor. Problem is, how
do we know we're doing the right things—or doing them
enough? Every religion has different requirements!

But Christian faith is different. It's spelled D-O-N-E.
The primary focus isn't on us trying to do righteous things.
Christianity is based on the merciful things Jesus has done
for us—washing "away our sins, giving us a new birth and
new life through the Holy Spirit."

Let's spell it out clearly: we can't E-A-R-N salvation;
it's a G-I-F-T.

*Thou didst seek us when we sought not Thee,
didst seek us indeed that we might seek Thee.*

AUGUSTINE OF HIPPO

HE UNDERSTANDS

*Since he himself has gone through suffering and testing,
he is able to help us when we are being tested.*

HEBREWS 2:18

When you experience deep family strife, when your friends and those you trust desert you, do you solicit advice from your twelve-year-old neighbor?

No! When trouble comes, you want to pick the brain of someone who has been through those ordeals and lived to tell the tale, someone who has had time to gain wisdom from the trials in his or her life.

This is the point being made by the writer of Hebrews. In Jesus Christ, the God-man, we have a Savior who knows firsthand about life's struggles, trials, and temptations. He doesn't just spout *theories* about these things. He has real-life experience—and a sterling track record—in such situations.

Call on Jesus. He understands. He is able to help.

*You don't really know Jesus is all you
need until Jesus is all you have.*

TIMOTHY KELLER

IT'S WORTH IT

Let's not get tired of doing what is good. At just the right time we will reap a harvest of blessing if we don't give up.

GALATIANS 6:9

A high school teacher endures draining days, turns in countless lesson plans, attends long faculty meetings, grades incessantly, and cares for the individual needs of dozens of students every year. All this without adequate pay or appreciation.

It doesn't seem worth it most days. But let the teacher hang in there faithfully for thirty years. If he or she does, thousands of kids will have been impacted.

This is Paul's point. When we pour into people for the sake of Jesus, when we refuse to quit, over time we make a huge, eternal difference.

Today, don't get tired of doing what is good. Don't give up! It's worth it.

It is better to wear out than to rust out.

GEORGE WHITEFIELD

LEARNING TO HUSTLE

*Lazy people want much but get little, but
those who work hard will prosper.*

PROVERBS 13:4

They're not called "the Greatest Generation" for nothing.

With many born just before the "Roaring 20s," they came of age during the Great Depression of the thirties. Still kids, they were then called upon in the forties to fight a worldwide war. After the horrors of World War II, they came home, started families, and built businesses that made the American economy the greatest on earth.

Many of this generation were courageous and creative, resourceful and resilient. But basically they were hardworking. They hustled, sometimes working two and three jobs to provide for their families and make ends meet, just like many must do today. As a result they experienced the truth of Solomon's words above.

Trust the words of Solomon, and like the Greatest Generation, honor God today with a solid work ethic.

Fear God and work hard.
DAVID LIVINGSTONE

YES, YOU CAN

I can do everything through Christ, who gives me strength.

PHILIPPIANS 4:13

Which situation would cause you to throw up your hands and cry, "I can't": Being jobless? Homeless? Falsely accused and jailed? Betrayed by friends? Becoming the long-term caregiver for an ailing family member?

In what was basically a thank-you note to the Christians at Philippi for their financial support, the apostle Paul claimed, "I can do everything."

He had been writing about his crazy missionary life—how alternating times of poverty and plenty had helped him learn contentment. In essence he said, "Whatever God gives me to face or calls me to accomplish is okay. *Because of Christ*, I can do it."

Today, tune out all the voices that say, "No, you can't." Listen to the one who says, "In me, you can."

Whatever Christ has for you to do, He will supply the power.

J. VERNON MCGEE

THE EYES OF THE LORD

*The LORD keeps watch over you as you
come and go, both now and forever.*

PSALM 121:8

Scopophobia is the overwhelming and irrational fear of being stared at or watched. These days, the fear of being watched grips more than just paranoid people. Government agencies monitor personal e-mails. Hackers routinely hijack unsecured webcams. Security cameras are *everywhere*. "Big brother" is definitely watching.

Fortunately, so is God. He "keeps watch over" his people, the psalmist declares. This verb can also be translated as "observes, heeds, guards, cares for." God is actually our heavenly watchman.

Knowing that the Lord keeps watch over you ought to elicit two responses: (1) It should cause you to rest easy. The Lord is with you in all circumstances. (2) It should motivate you to live righteously. You're never hidden from the eyes of the Lord.

*A God wise enough to create me and the world
I live in is wise enough to watch out for me.*

PHILIP YANCEY

BAD NEWS/GOOD NEWS

All of us, like sheep, have strayed away.
We have left God's paths to follow our own.
Yet the LORD laid on him the sins of us all.

ISAIAH 53:6

This well-known verse says something bad about us and something good about God.

What it says about us is sobering. We humans stray like sheep. We willfully abandon the way of God and go our independent way. In short, we are guilty of sin.

But look at the breathtaking truth this verse reveals about God. The Lord has "laid on him [i.e., the Messiah/ Christ] the sins of us all."

Take a few minutes to read all of Isaiah 53. In the words of one old Texas cowboy, "If that doesn't ring your bell, your clapper's broke."

My memory is nearly gone. But I remember two things: that
I am a great sinner, and that Christ is a great Saviour.

JOHN NEWTON

SECRET WEAPON

I have hidden your word in my heart,
that I might not sin against you.

PSALM 119:11

Mention memorizing Scripture, and many Christians protest, "Oh, I could *never* do that! I have a *terrible* memory."

Not true. Think of the information we've got tucked away—song lyrics, computer passwords, birthdays, sports statistics, and so on. Few of us can claim a photographic memory, but we can at least remember most things we want to remember.

When we know God's Word by heart, we can take it with us everywhere, pull it out anytime, ponder it in any situation, or use it to fight any temptation. The idea is that God's truth will seep down from our heads into our hearts. Once it takes root there, it can bring forth good fruit.

Why not start now with this verse?

The Bible will keep you from sin, or sin
will keep you from the Bible.

D. L. MOODY

MOSTLY DEAD?

I lie in the dust; revive me by your word.

PSALM 119:25

Near the end of the classic movie *The Princess Bride*, it appears the hero of the story has died. Westley's comrades carry his lifeless body to a wizard named Miracle Max who announces good news: their friend is only "mostly dead."

It's a funny scene, but "mostly dead" is not a fun feeling, lying in the dust of a crumbling life, wondering if you still have a pulse.

If you're in that place, hear the good news: God is willing and able to revive you. Draw near to him. Open his Word. Listen to his voice. Cling to his promises. As you do this faithfully, you will sense life flowing into your "mostly dead" soul.

Christians in revival are accordingly found living
in God's presence . . . attending to His Word.

J. I. PACKER

THE MESSES WE MAKE WITH OUR MOUTHS

Take control of what I say, O LORD, and guard my lips.

PSALM 141:3

Which seems better to you: lying in bed tonight lamenting all the wrong things you blurted out today or thanking God for all the dumb things you *didn't* say (and the good things you did)?

The point? We can use our mouths as deadly weapons, or we can use them to "bring healing" (Proverbs 12:18).

In light of this sobering truth, pray the short but great prayer of David above. Then determine, by the enabling power of God's Spirit, to use your mouth "as an instrument to do what is right for the glory of God" (Romans 6:13). Ask the Spirit to "elbow" you in the heart every time you start to say something unnecessary or hurtful.

Nothing is almost always a good thing to say.

UNKNOWN

THORNS AND WEEDS

The seed that fell on good soil represents those who hear and accept God's word and produce a harvest of thirty, sixty, or even a hundred times as much as had been planted!

MARK 4:20

In his parable about the farmer scattering seed, Jesus warned about having an infertile heart where the seed of the gospel cannot produce fruit.

This means you ponder God's Word and it rings true. Something in you wants to obey it. But you close your Bible, leave church, and immediately you're worrying about the things of this world, or you just plain forget what you heard. Next week it's the same drill. Nothing ever changes.

Your best hope? Ask Jesus to help you do a little weeding. Once Jesus has made your heart into good soil, the seeds will grow, thrive, and bear fruit.

In our hearts, the weeds of sin are plentiful; but there is one who will take care to pluck up evil growths.

CHARLES H. SPURGEON

MINISTRY OF MESSIAH

*The Spirit of the LORD is upon me, for he has anointed
me to bring Good News to the poor. He has sent
me to proclaim that captives will be released, that
the blind will see, that the oppressed will be set free,
and that the time of the LORD's favor has come.*

LUKE 4:18-19

After reading this passage from Isaiah during a synagogue service in his hometown, Jesus claimed these messianic promises applied to himself.

While anyone can claim anything, Jesus backed up his claims. He taught liberating truth to the poor. He set free those at the mercy of demons and illnesses and addictions. He gave sight to the blind.

It was "the time of the LORD's favor." It still is.

*Make ready for the Christ, whose smile, like
lightning, sets free the song of everlasting glory that
now sleeps, in your paper flesh, like dynamite.*

THOMAS MERTON

ONE MEDIATOR

There is one God and one Mediator who can reconcile
God and humanity—the man Christ Jesus.

1 TIMOTHY 2:5

A *mediator* is a go-between who works to reconcile serious disagreements between two or more parties. When a skilled mediator gains the full trust of each side, reconciliation typically follows.

This verse says that Jesus Christ is the "one Mediator" between a holy God and a rebellious human race. Fully God and fully man, the tempted yet sinless Jesus satisfied the Father even as he showed his love for sinners. Only his life, death, and resurrection can reconcile sinners to God.

No one else can stand in the gap—and bridge the gap—between God and humankind. Ask the Lord to open the eyes of those who are seeking to be reconciled to God in other, futile ways.

They who have not this one God by one Mediator, have none.

A. R. FAUSSET

DARK VALLEYS

Even when I walk through the darkest valley,
I will not be afraid, for you are close beside me.
Your rod and your staff protect and comfort me.

PSALM 23:4

Sheep aren't the fiercest of God's creatures. Who gets mauled by a ewe or trampled by a lamb? Sheep are also not terribly quick.

When you are not ferocious, nor fast, then you are highly vulnerable. Predators call sheep without a shepherd "dinner."

In this psalm, we're compared to sheep. Yet we're not at risk—the Lord is our shepherd. He's with us through all the dark valleys of life. With his rod he beats back would-be predators. With his staff—and its crook—he guides us and pulls us out of danger.

Today, instead of fearing all that's "out there," put your faith in the one who's right here.

Death is a king of terrors, but not to the sheep of Christ.
MATTHEW HENRY

HELP IN PRAYER

*The Holy Spirit helps us in our weakness. For
example, we don't know what God wants us to
pray for. But the Holy Spirit prays for us with
groanings that cannot be expressed in words.*

ROMANS 8:26

Sometimes we can't see or understand what God is up to
in our lives. We don't even know how to pray. All these
swirling feelings, competing desires, and weary questions
flood our hearts, yet we can't find words to express them.

It's in such times that we receive divine help. In the
words of Tim Keller, the Spirit "makes our groaning *his*
groaning, putting his prayers to the Father inside our
prayers."

Are you struggling to pray today? The indwelling
Spirit of God is praying *for you*!

*The right way to approach God is to stretch out our hands
and ask of One who we know has the heart of a Father.*

DIETRICH BONHOEFFER

CHILDREN OF GOD

*To all who believed him and accepted him, he
gave the right to become children of God.*

JOHN 1:12

"We're *all* children of God." We hear this sentiment
often. It's a nice, inclusive idea. Unfortunately, it isn't
what the Bible teaches.

Though God is the *creator* of all, the apostle John
says here that God is a *father* only to those who believe
and accept Christ.

This means when we trust Jesus' words and character
enough to "grasp or take hold of" him (that's another
way to translate the Greek word translated *accept* in this
verse), then and only then does he grant us the right to
claim the title "child of God."

This kind of "grasping" belief is like the difference
between merely reading about ropes in a book and hanging by a rope over the edge of a cliff.

[Grace is] free sovereign favor to the ill-deserving.

B. B. WARFIELD

BIG HELP FOR BIG UNDERTAKINGS

On October 2 the wall was finished—just fifty-two days after we had begun. When our enemies and the surrounding nations heard about it, they were frightened and humiliated. They realized this work had been done with the help of our God.

NEHEMIAH 6:15-16

Nehemiah was a pencil-pushing government employee, not an engineer. Nevertheless, when he heard the walls of Jerusalem were in ruins, he got busy.

He leveraged his connections, returned home from Persia, assembled his demoralized fellow Jews, and lit a fire under them. With courageous effort and continual prayer, he led regular folks (not professional wall builders) in completing a massive task—against fierce opposition—in less than two months.

Can you say, "Wow!"? Never doubt what God can do through regular people who trust in him.

God's work, done in God's way, will never lack God's supplies.

HUDSON TAYLOR

UNITED WITH CHRIST

My old self has been crucified with Christ. It is no longer I who live, but Christ lives in me. So I live in this earthly body by trusting in the Son of God, who loved me and gave himself for me.

GALATIANS 2:20

One of the most prominent but challenging truths of Christian theology to grasp is the teaching that believers are *united with Christ*.

The idea is that by God's grace and through our faith, believers share fully in Christ's death, resurrection, righteousness, and new life.

Among other things, this means that when Jesus died on the cross, in a mysterious yet real way, we (i.e., our old selves) died too. When he conquered sin and death, his victory became ours.

You are one with Christ! Live today by trusting fully in the one who lives in you.

We ought not to separate Christ from ourselves or ourselves from him.

JOHN CALVIN

THE ANSWER IS . . .

*We do this by keeping our eyes on Jesus, the champion who
initiates and perfects our faith. Because of the joy awaiting
him, he endured the cross, disregarding its shame. Now
he is seated in the place of honor beside God's throne.*

HEBREWS 12:2

If we were playing the popular game show *Jeopardy!*,
we'd give this question to the answer in the verse above:
"How do we keep living by faith in a confusing and cruel
world?"

Maybe life's like that for you right now. Like the
original readers of the book of Hebrews, you're spiritually adrift, in danger of sinking.

If so, here's your hope: look to Jesus. Do this, not
merely because he's a great example of trust and endurance. Do it because he's the champion who initiates and
perfects your faith.

*Faith means trusting in advance what
will make sense only in reverse.*

PHILIP YANCEY

A MURDEROUS HEART

This is the message you have heard from the beginning:
We should love one another. We must not be like Cain,
who belonged to the evil one and killed his brother.

1 JOHN 3:11-12

People love to refer to these verses from 1 John because they remind us of how crucial the condition of our hearts is.

We all know and accept that murder is wrong, but we would do well to remember that it is also wrong to murder someone in our hearts, by hating them, by being jealous of them.

The command is simple: love one another. If we always choose love, we will never be in danger of being like Cain.

If I prayed God that all men should approve of my conduct,
I should find myself a penitent at the door of each one, but
I shall rather pray that my heart may be pure towards all.

SARAH, DESERT MOTHER

WITNESSES

You will receive power when the Holy Spirit comes upon you. And you will be my witnesses, telling people about me everywhere—in Jerusalem, throughout Judea, in Samaria, and to the ends of the earth.

ACTS 1:8

Just before returning to heaven, Jesus gave these marching orders to his followers. Notice how clear he was:

Who? *You*

What? *Be my witnesses* (i.e., tell what you've seen, heard, experienced)

When? *When the Holy Spirit comes* (for us this happens when we trust Jesus)

Where? *Everywhere*

Why? Because *people* must know what Jesus did for them

How? Through the *power* the Spirit gives

A witness simply shares Christ in the power of God's Spirit. *You* can do that.

Dost thou see a soul that has the image of God in him? Love him, love him; say, "This man and I must go to heaven one day."

JOHN BUNYAN

---

*Jesus replied, "'You must love the LORD your God
with all your heart, all your soul, and all your mind.'
This is the first and greatest commandment. A second is
equally important: 'Love your neighbor as yourself.'"*

MATTHEW 22:37-39

The Jewish religious leaders wrangled over the 613 dos
and don'ts of the Mosaic law the way sports fans argue
over Hall of Fame players: Which one towers over all
the rest?

When one leader asked Jesus this divisive question,
Jesus boiled the whole law down to this ingenious two-
part answer: love God supremely; love others sacrificially.

You'd have to admit, life *does* go better when we live
that way. How can you show your love to God and to a
neighbor today?

*Every Christian would agree that a man's spiritual
health is exactly proportional to his love for God.*

C. S. LEWIS

LIFE-CHANGING TRUTH

Make them holy by your truth;
teach them your word, which is truth.

JOHN 17:17

What's Jesus praying for here? For us to just read the Bible more often so that we'd stop sinning?

Quiet times aren't spiritual antibiotics. We can't just ingest a few verses, then discover in a day or two that our sin is cleared up like a minor infection. We need daily infusions from God's Word. It needs to permeate our entire being. Only then will we be immune to the enemy's crippling lies.

It's sort of like this book. You may find certain discussions of particular verses helpful. But if you *really* want to be healthy and holy long term, you need much more truth than a quick devotional thought.

Make Jesus' prayer your own. Substitute "me" for "them." Then dig deeply into God's Word.

If you cut him, he'd bleed Scripture!
CHARLES H. SPURGEON,
SPEAKING OF JOHN BUNYAN

FEAR OR FAITH?

Fearing people is a dangerous trap,
but trusting the LORD means safety.

PROVERBS 29:25

Sam is at a social function, and her mind is consumed by one thought: *What do these people think of me?*

Self-conscious about her appearance and too terrified to say or do *anything* for fear of how people might respond, Sam's basically frozen. *Why did I even come? I wish I were invisible!*

Fearing people is a miserable way to go through life. The alternative is to trust the Lord, to rest in his arms. He knows all your flaws, and still, he's crazy about you. You're always safe with him.

Until we let this truth set us free, we'll remain stuck in the "fearing people" trap.

The remarkable thing about fearing God is that
when you fear God you fear nothing else, whereas
if you do not fear God you fear everything else.

OSWALD CHAMBERS

CHASING SHEEP

The LORD is my shepherd; I have all that I need.

PSALM 23:1

David could have used words like "King" or "Judge" to describe the One who provides for him. But in this popular verse, he likened Yahweh to a *shepherd*.

A shepherd leads, feeds, and protects a flock of sheep. It's a messy job because dim-witted sheep routinely wander off into muck and mire. And guess who gets to fetch them when they do.

Back in the day, shepherding was also a full-time occupation, not a part-time gig. The phrase *clocking out* wasn't part of the vernacular.

Depicting God Almighty as a *shepherd* is breathtaking enough, but look closely at what David declared: "The LORD is *my* shepherd" (emphasis added).

Those five words, if taken to heart, change everything about how we view God and how we view ourselves in light of his nonstop care for us.

Complete happiness is knowing God.

JOHN CALVIN

NERVES AND FAITH

The LORD will work out his plans for my life—
for your faithful love, O LORD, endures forever.
Don't abandon me, for you made me.

PSALM 138:8

Hedley Donovan, former editor in chief at Time, Inc., once confessed, "Things will probably come out all right, but sometimes it takes strong nerves just to watch."

We nod. We've been there. We've all had nerve-racking moments. Yet as God's people, we have divine assurances that everything *will* come out all right. Why, then, do we cringe and doubt our way through life?

We're in good company. Look at David. One moment he's confident: "The LORD will work out his plans for my life" (no "probably" there). The next he's asking God not to abandon him!

Strong nerves are a normal part of life, but strong faith will serve us better.

Even in the life of a Christian, faith rises and
falls like the tides of an invisible sea.

FLANNERY O'CONNOR

"AS I HAVE LOVED"

*Now I am giving you a new commandment: Love each
other. Just as I have loved you, you should love each other.*

JOHN 13:34

If only Jesus had stopped speaking after saying, "Love
each other." It's easy to find cover in vagueness. Where
details lack, excuses can flourish.

But Jesus kept going. He clarified his sweeping command by adding, "Just as I have loved you."

Gulp. In other words, love unconditionally, sacrificially, tenaciously, graciously, lavishly, eternally.

Astute readers will no doubt think, *But that's
impossible*—which is probably why John came back later
and reminded believers that "love comes from God"
(1 John 4:7).

When we're all out of love, God's got an endless
supply.

*May my love for my fellow men grow deeper and more tender,
and may I be more willing to take their burdens upon myself.*

JOHN BAILLIE

THE MARK OF
THE CHRISTIAN

---

*Your love for one another will prove to the
world that you are my disciples.*

JOHN 13:35

In writing about this famous statement by Jesus, the late,
great theologian Francis A. Schaeffer called brotherly love
among believers "the mark of the Christian."

Schaeffer argued that when believers bicker, when
our lives are marked by fighting and friction, when our
congregations crack apart, the world has every right—
based on this one verse alone—to question our claim that
we are followers of Jesus.

Let this sobering verse prompt you to do some
prayerful soul searching. How are your relationships? Are
they marked by grace and truth? Forgiveness? Humility
and service? Kindness? Generosity?

Do something concrete to show love today.

*Love—and the unity it attests to—is the mark Christ gave
Christians to wear before the world. Only with this mark
may the world know that Christians are indeed Christians.*

FRANCIS A. SCHAEFFER

ONE FACE

People with integrity walk safely, but those who
follow crooked paths will be exposed.

PROVERBS 10:9

Integrity means "wholeness, blamelessness, the state of
being without defect."

People with integrity don't act one way today and a
different way tomorrow. They don't have different per-
sonas that they put on and take off like clothing. No,
people of integrity consistently display good character,
even when no one's watching. With them, what you see
is what you get, all the time.

One of the many great advantages of integrity is
safety. So long as your commitment is *always* to say and
do the right, God-honoring thing, you never have to
worry about getting caught in a lie or a scandal.

No man, for any considerable period, can wear one face
to himself and another to the multitude, without finally
getting bewildered as to which may be the true.

NATHANIEL HAWTHORNE

UNCEASING

*The faithful love of the LORD never ends! His
mercies never cease. Great is his faithfulness;
his mercies begin afresh each morning.*

LAMENTATIONS 3:22-23

The day before vacation, you're reminded of why you
want to escape in the first place: a new headache at work,
a fresh batch of bills, some bad news from a friend,
reports of another terrorist attack. Don't the problems
ever stop?

Two days later you're walking along the beach at
dawn, mesmerized by the unique beauty of a new day,
in awe of the churning surf. You see that glorious sun-
rise. You can feel those waves breaking at your feet like
clockwork. One after another, they just keep coming.
Suddenly you're thinking of this verse.

Though it seems sorrows and trials won't ever stop,
God's love and mercy are truly unceasing.

*The same Everlasting Father Who cares for you to-day,
will take care of you to-morrow, and every day.*

FRANCIS DE SALES

PRAYING LIKE PAUL

*I pray that from his glorious, unlimited resources
he will empower you with inner strength through
his Spirit. Then Christ will make his home in your
hearts as you trust in him. Your roots will grow
down into God's love and keep you strong.*

EPHESIANS 3:16-17

It's passages like this one that prompted eminent Bible scholar Martyn Lloyd-Jones to say of Ephesians, "There is nothing more sublime in the whole range of Scripture than this Epistle."

If you think that's an exaggeration, look again closely at Paul's words. Notice what they say about our triune God and what he longs to do for and in us. Indulge your holy imagination. What if your life mirrored this description?

Finally do this: make this prayer your own. Then pray it for everyone you encounter.

*Every great movement of God can be
traced to a kneeling figure.*

D. L. MOODY

HEADS, HEARTS, AND HANDS

Teach me your ways, O LORD, that I may live according to your truth! Grant me purity of heart, so that I may honor you.

PSALM 86:11

Many believers take a "head and hands" approach to the spiritual life. They focus exclusively on "knowing and doing God's truth." While knowledge and obedience are indispensable, if that's *all* you've got going for you, you might end up becoming a Pharisee!

More than head and hands, we also need to focus on our hearts. This is the origin of our life's direction (Proverbs 4:23). It's why David prayed, "Grant me purity of heart, so that I may honor you."

Even when we love God, other loves can creep in and divide our hearts. Since your desire is to honor God, make David's prayer *your* prayer.

We know truth, not only by the reason, but also by the heart.

BLAISE PASCAL

THE GREAT EXCHANGE

God made Christ, who never sinned, to be the offering for our sin, so that we could be made right with God through Christ.

2 CORINTHIANS 5:21

Here's a strong piece of evidence that Christianity is true: If you were going to make up a religion, could you ever come up with anything like the gospel? The Creator of everything entered his own creation, the infinite becoming finite—fully God *and* fully man. He was on a divine rescue mission to turn enemies into beloved children. The innocent one suffered for the guilty, and the Author of life died in order to give life to the dead. The sinless one took humanity's sin upon himself so that he can give his righteousness to the unrighteous. All to bring all creation into a renewed relationship with our Creator.

It's the ultimate exchange: righteousness for sin and life for death. By faith, have you swapped your failure for Jesus' perfect success?

You contribute nothing to your salvation except the sin that made it necessary.

JONATHAN EDWARDS

FULLY COMMITTED

*The eyes of the LORD search the whole earth in order to
strengthen those whose hearts are fully committed to him.
What a fool you have been! From now on you will be at war.*

2 CHRONICLES 16:9

King Asa of Judah acted foolishly. Needing military protection, he turned to the Syrian king Ben-hadad instead of to the Lord his God. Consequently God sent Hanani the seer with this sobering message.

What was grim news for Asa is great news for us. Hanani's words tell us that God doesn't merely glance down from heaven on occasion. He searches the whole earth for people whose hearts are fully committed to him. When he finds them, he strengthens them.

Are you facing trouble? Resist the urge to turn to substitute saviors. Trust exclusively in God. He's looking to pour his power into your devoted heart.

Of all cares, which go beyond bounds, unbelief is the mother.

JOHN CALVIN

BLESSED TO BLESS

*He ensures that orphans and widows receive
justice. He shows love to the foreigners living
among you and gives them food and clothing.*

DEUTERONOMY 10:18

From the very beginning, God's message to his people
was this: I will bless you so that you will be a blessing to
the world (Genesis 12:1-3). This was Israel's job description: show the world what a great God you serve; be holy
and live with compassion.

This is the church's job description too. Don't just
moralize. Make a difference! Instead of spending all your
time talking about spiritual truth, join God's work in
transforming the world with it. Care for those in need.
Feed an orphan. Check on a widow. Help convicts get
back on their feet. Stand up for the oppressed. Work for
justice.

*The followers of Jesus are children of God, and they
should manifest the family likeness by doing good to all.*

F. F. BRUCE

WORKING OUT YOUR SALVATION

Dear friends, you always followed my instructions
when I was with you. And now that I am away, it is
even more important. Work hard to show the results
of your salvation, obeying God with deep reverence
and fear. For God is working in you, giving you the
desire and the power to do what pleases him.

PHILIPPIANS 2:12-13

We don't work *for* our salvation. But we are called to work hard to show it.

That means our role in the spiritual life is to respond to God, to repent of sin, to trust and obey God's commands. All of that is active, not passive. All of that takes effort on our part.

Meanwhile, God is working too. In fact, he *always* does his part. The only question is, will we do ours?

Holiness is not a condition that we drift into.

JOHN STOTT

BURSTING OUT!

*The LORD is my strength and shield. I trust him with
all my heart. He helps me, and my heart is filled
with joy. I burst out in songs of thanksgiving.*

PSALM 28:7

Remember the kids' chorus "If You're Happy and You
Know It"? That's David in this psalm. Can't you just see
him clapping his hands, stomping his feet, and shouting,
"Hallelujah!"?

God, in his goodness, gives us times like this—when
we sense his presence, our faith is strong, our hearts are
full, and joy flows like a mountain spring.

If that's you today, bless God! Put on some praise
choruses and sing with all your might. And if that's not
you today, go ahead and do the same exact thing!

*Feelings come and go, and when they come a good use can
be made of them: they cannot be our regular spiritual diet.*

C. S. LEWIS

OCTOBER 23

THINKING STRAIGHT

---

*Dear brothers and sisters, one final thing. Fix your
thoughts on what is true, and honorable, and right,
and pure, and lovely, and admirable. Think about
things that are excellent and worthy of praise.*

PHILIPPIANS 4:8

We live in a world where almost everything is beyond our
control. We can't orchestrate events or determine outcomes. Nor can we dictate the actions of others.

One thing we *can* control, however (only with God's
help, of course), is our thoughts.

We get to choose our thoughts. We can entertain
untrue ideas, focusing on what's negative and dark. Or
we can follow Paul's counsel in this encouraging verse and
think on the true and good.

Where will you fix your thoughts today?

*You are either in the Word and the Word is conforming
you to the image of Jesus Christ, or you are in the
world and the world is squeezing you into its mold.*

HOWARD HENDRICKS

FLOOD OF JUSTICE

*I want to see a mighty flood of justice, an
endless river of righteous living.*

AMOS 5:24

Jeremiah may have been the "weeping prophet." But
Amos? Not so much. Maybe it was just his personality.
Whatever the reason, Amos's tone was tough; his words
hit his listeners like a two-by-four right between the eyes.
He hammered Israel's wealthy, religious crowd for ignoring the downtrodden even as they feigned deep devotion
to God.

God doesn't want his people clustered in holier-than-
thou huddles. He wants us building a society where those
who hurt can experience his love. He wants us actively
engaged in righting wrongs—both personal and societal.

Where does God's justice need to flow in and through
your life?

*A private faith that does not act in the face
of oppression is no faith at all.*

CHARLES COLSON

THE TROUBLE WITH TROUBLE

Don't let your hearts be troubled.
Trust in God, and trust also in me.

JOHN 14:1

Troubled heart describes some people all the time, and all people some of the time.

Already stirred up over an issue at home, you arrive at work only to find a disturbing situation awaiting you. Following an agitating drive home, you watch disconcerting stories on the news.

It's a troubled world, but we don't have to allow that trouble to invade our hearts. Rather than succumbing to fear and curling up in the fetal position, how about we get on our knees?

Remember: faith isn't a feeling. It's choosing to place our confidence in the Lord's power, presence, and promises.

It is of no use to say to men, "Let not your hearts
be troubled," unless you finish the verse and say,
"Believe in God, believe also in Christ."

ALEXANDER MACLAREN

NO OTHER NAME

There is salvation in no one else! God has given no other name under heaven by which we must be saved.

ACTS 4:12

"You Christians are arrogant to claim that Jesus is the only way to God! How can you be so narrow and bigoted?"

This common accusation is worth talking about. A few truths for our skeptical friends: (1) We are only repeating what Christ himself said (John 14:6). (2) To the extent that we have been arrogant in sharing Christ's message, we need to ask for forgiveness! (3) It's true the gospel is narrow and exclusive. But instead of being angry about that, think of it this way: If, while dying of thirst, you came across a well, would it make more sense to rant, "Why aren't there ten wells?" or would it be wiser to just take a drink?

The truth does not change according to our ability to stomach it.

FLANNERY O'CONNOR

NEW HEARTS

---

*I will give you a new heart, and I will put a new
spirit in you. I will take out your stony, stubborn
heart and give you a tender, responsive heart.*

EZEKIEL 36:26

Israel's history was checkered with hard-hearted rebellion. Despite remarkable grace and patience from the one true God, the people chased after lesser, false gods.

Here the prophet spoke of a day when God would do much more than give laws inscribed on stone. He would give his people new hearts.

We know this by experience: rules and threats can sometimes coerce people into compliance, but the moment external pressure is gone, look out! Lasting change requires genuine, internal transformation in character.

Thank God *this* is what the gospel offers—not just more rules, but new hearts with new desires.

*The solution to sin is not to impose an ever-
stricter code of behavior. It is to know God.*

PHILIP YANCEY

WORK AS WORSHIP

*Work willingly at whatever you do, as though you were
working for the Lord rather than for people. Remember
that the Lord will give you an inheritance as your
reward, and that the Master you are serving is Christ.*

COLOSSIANS 3:23-24

Some people worship their work. It consumes them.
They give themselves utterly to advancing in a career.

Other people worship *by* their work. They see their
job as an opportunity to shine for Christ. They use their
gifts and abilities to serve customers and coworkers for
the glory of God.

Consider the chores Jesus likely completed as a child,
those items he may have made as a carpenter during his
young adult years. God is, it would seem, as pleased by a
well-made plow as he is by a well-spoken parable.

*No matter what I do . . . I am to do it as if I'm doing
it for God, and so it becomes an act of worship.*

RICK WARREN

READY TO HELP

God is our refuge and strength, always
ready to help in times of trouble.

PSALM 46:1

When troubles come, there's no end to the places people run.

We seek refuge in relationships, projects, substances, and entertainment. Or we look to shopping, sleep, food, sex, work, hobbies, exercise, vacation, ad infinitum.

Experience shows that we never get lasting help in any of these places. At most we find distraction and a little bit of short-term relief.

The psalmist got it right. Only God is a true refuge. Ultimate safety and strength are found in him.

If you think, "This verse is only for people like Mother Teresa or Billy Graham. God would never help someone like *me*," notice what it says: "God is . . . always ready to help."

They, who have God for their God, are safe . . . they
have his faithful promise to be their refuge.
JONATHAN EDWARDS

TRUE WORSHIP

Dear brothers and sisters, I plead with you to give your bodies to God because of all he has done for you. Let them be a living and holy sacrifice—the kind he will find acceptable. This is truly the way to worship him.

ROMANS 12:1

After spending eleven chapters extolling all the wonderful things God has done through Christ to forgive us and bring us to himself, Paul issues a well-known challenge. Give yourself completely to God. Be a living sacrifice. Make your life one continuous worship service.

Whether you did this yesterday is irrelevant. Is this your heart's stance *today*?

Offer up your time and energy to him. Align all your efforts and desires, possessions and plans, thoughts and dreams to his good will for your life.

The problem with a living sacrifice is that it keeps crawling off the altar.

D. L. MOODY

OCTOBER 31

DIVINE SUPPLY

*This same God who takes care of me will supply
all your needs from his glorious riches, which
have been given to us in Christ Jesus.*

PHILIPPIANS 4:19

In Paul's letter to the Philippian believers, we find this comforting promise: "God . . . will supply all your needs." There's nothing complex about it: if we have a need, we can trust God to supply it. And no need is too great since the infinite God has made his glorious riches available to us in Christ Jesus.

Whatever your need is—whether financial, physical, emotional, social, marital—bring it to God, then trust his word.

And if God *doesn't* give you what you request, know that in his wise estimation he will provide otherwise.

He gave a checkbook with this one condition,
"You never can draw more than you need at the time."

A. B. SIMPSON

STARRY, STARRY NIGHT

Abram believed the LORD, and the LORD counted
him as righteous because of his faith.

GENESIS 15:6

As Abram looked at the night sky, God repeated his promise that a miracle baby would be born to the childless, aging couple: Abram (i.e., Abraham) and his wife, Sarai (i.e., Sarah).

For dramatic effect God added, "Look up into the sky and count the stars if you can. That's how many descendants you will have!" (Genesis 15:5).

Abram might have smirked or mumbled sarcastically, "That's exactly what you told me *ten years ago*." Instead he trusted God, and the doorways of his faith opened. What blessings came Abraham's way (and ours!) because he believed.

That's still how God works. So trust him. Wait to see what he will do and how your faith will end up blessing others.

God makes a promise. Faith believes it.
Hope anticipates it. Patience quietly awaits it.

D. L. MOODY

NOVEMBER 2

ONE SURE WAY

*Jesus told him, "I am the way, the truth, and the life.
No one can come to the Father except through me."*

JOHN 14:6

According to Jesus, the only way to get to God is "through" Jesus. Could he have said anything more controversial? Our tolerant age tolerates almost anything—except exclusive statements like this.

The interesting thing is that this *isn't* a negative announcement; it's wonderfully good news. Jesus is the way to God. The worst sinner on earth can come to God through Jesus. So what if there aren't five hundred ways to God? There's one sure way, and it's open to all!

Pray for the people in your life who have yet to put their faith in Jesus. Ask God for opportunities to "show and tell" them this good news.

*You have nothing to do but to save souls.
Therefore spend and be spent in this work.*

JOHN WESLEY

CHRIST'S BRIDE

*All the believers devoted themselves to the apostles'
teaching, and to fellowship, and to sharing in meals
(including the Lord's Supper), and to prayer.*

ACTS 2:42

This verse is the best snapshot we have of the early church.

Luke notes how those first Christians "worshiped together at the Temple" and met regularly in homes (Acts 2:46). They witnessed miracles and exuded joy. The result? "Each day the Lord added to their fellowship those who were being saved" (verse 47).

The New Testament refers to the church as the "bride" of Christ (2 Corinthians 11:2; Revelation 22:17; see also Ephesians 5:21-33), and from the beginning, believers have been called to the following:

- Worship—living for the glory of God
- Instruction—learning the truth of God
- Fellowship—loving the people of God
- Evangelism—leading the lost to God

Is this your "wifely" focus too?

The Creator arranged things so that we need each other.

BASIL OF CAESAREA

FULL OF GRACE AND TRUTH

*The LORD detests lying lips, but he delights
in those who tell the truth.*

PROVERBS 12:22

"The God of truth" (Isaiah 65:16) whose "words are truth" (2 Samuel 7:28)—the same one who sent Jesus, the embodiment of truth (see John 14:6, to set us free with truth (John 8:32), and who then sent the "Spirit of truth" to live in Christians (John 15:26)—says here, "I hate lying."

We can be quick to protest: "I don't lie!" But do we tell that little white lie? Do we repeat the rumor? Do we exaggerate the story? Do we fudge our taxes?

John described Jesus as being full of "grace and truth" (John 1:17, NIV). May we be just like our Lord, and may he delight in us.

*A lie will go round the world while
truth is pulling its boots on.*

CHARLES H. SPURGEON

MAN'S EXTREMITY, GOD'S OPPORTUNITY

O our God, won't you stop them? We are powerless against this mighty army that is about to attack us. We do not know what to do, but we are looking to you for help.

2 CHRONICLES 20:12

When Jehoshaphat was king, God's people in Judah were once attacked by *three* enemy armies.

Rather than hitting the panic button, Jehoshaphat called on people to hit their knees. When they did—in faith—they experienced a miraculous deliverance.

We generally cringe at difficulties. We typically see prayer as a last resort. In God's economy, however, it's trouble that sparks earnest prayer and it's prayer that is the prelude to something wonderful. Matthew Henry's observation was dead-on: "When God intends to bless His people, the first thing He does is to set them a-praying."

We have to pray with our eyes on God, not on the difficulties.

OSWALD CHAMBERS

LOCKED OUT?

---

*Look! I stand at the door and knock. If you hear
my voice and open the door, I will come in, and
we will share a meal together as friends.*

REVELATION 3:20

This famous verse is typically used by Christians in sharing the gospel. We tell unbelievers, "See here? Jesus is knocking on the door of your heart, and you need to let him in."

The problem with using this verse in this way? In Revelation 3, Jesus isn't addressing non-Christians; he's talking to church people!

Even those with true faith can drift from intimacy with Christ. We can fill our lives up with so many other things, and before long Christ is (so to speak) on the outside looking in. It's like that wise old saying: "If the Lord seems distant, it wasn't he who moved."

*We are at this moment as close to God
as we really choose to be.*

J. OSWALD SANDERS

HIDING IN GOD

The LORD is a shelter for the oppressed,
a refuge in times of trouble.

PSALM 9:9

Towering over dozens of Irish villages are ancient round towers. These stone structures, some over one hundred feet high, are believed to have been refuges for monks more than a thousand years ago. (Their winding staircases and tiny doorways were inaccessible to bigger, armor-wearing Viking invaders.)

This is the image conveyed in this beloved verse: *God* is our high tower. He's the fortress we can run to when life goes haywire. He doesn't magically eliminate our troubles—not even close. But we can hide *in him* during tough times. And, oh, do we ever learn about his character in those times.

If you're in a mess today, run to the one who is "a refuge in times of trouble."

Affliction is the best book in my library.
MARTIN LUTHER

BY THE HAND

The LORD directs the steps of the godly. He delights in
every detail of their lives. Though they stumble, they will
never fall, for the LORD holds them by the hand.

PSALM 37:23-24

Carl finds himself at a tough crossroads in life. He feels confused—even lost. God seems distant. Carl's nervous about proceeding, thinking, *What if I mess up?*

Carl needs the reassurances in this proclamation of David. He needs to remember what is true of God (instead of what seems true in his current situation): God is engaged and involved. He directs and delights in Carl's life. Carl can move forward with confidence, knowing God's got him.

Will Carl stumble? Sure. Will he fall and be destroyed? No way. Not when the Lord holds him by the hand.

How does this snapshot of God encourage you today, specifically?

Though our feelings come and go, His love for us does not.
C. S. LEWIS

BEING GRACED

He will not crush the weakest reed or put out a flickering candle. He will bring justice to all who have been wronged.

ISAIAH 42:3

In his bestselling book *What's So Amazing About Grace?* Philip Yancey tells the harrowing story of a desperate prostitute who was encouraged to go to a church for help. Her response is haunting: "Why would I ever go there? I was already feeling terrible about myself. They'd just make me feel worse."

According to Isaiah, this is *not* how the Messiah treats those who mess up. With him there's no berating, no shaming. "He will not crush the weakest reed." If you have just a flicker of life left, Jesus will restore you, not snuff you out.

What a great Savior! He looks on us with compassion, touches us with gentleness, rescues us with power.

I learned grace by being graced.
PHILIP YANCEY

MAKING DEAD THINGS LIVE

He asked me, "Son of man, can these bones
become living people again?" "O Sovereign LORD,"
I replied, "you alone know the answer to that."

EZEKIEL 37:3

In ancient Israel, nothing sucked the air out of a room like the arrival of a prophet of God. Imagine a job where your primary duty every day was to confront people with dire warnings and stern words!

This is why stories like the one in Ezekiel 37 are so refreshing. Here in the midst of all the doom and gloom is a vision of old bones in a desert coming to life again through the power of God.

Beyond the obvious application to Israel while in exile, it's a reminder of God's power, working to renew his people through the ages. He makes dead things—relationships, marriages, spiritually disinterested people—burst with new vitality. Ask him to do that in your life today.

There are three stages in every great work of God: first,
it is impossible, then it is difficult, then it is done.

HUDSON TAYLOR

"KNOW ME"

I want you to show love, not offer sacrifices. I want you to know me more than I want burnt offerings.

HOSEA 6:6

Despite God's constant goodness to them, the ancient Israelites had a bad habit of becoming less spiritually committed and more spiritually complacent. They frequently traded deep intimacy *with* God for religious activity *for* him, and finally stopped pursuing the Lord and started pursuing "god-substitutes."

We read the troubling story of the prophet Hosea marrying a prostitute—meant to be a picture of Israel's spiritual unfaithfulness—and we are shocked, wondering how God could ask such a thing.

But we modern-day believers have the same tendencies: to talk more about Jesus than we talk to him; to get bored with him and chase after other gods.

Read the verse again: God wants you to know him. He wants your heart.

We actually slander and dishonor God by our very eagerness to serve Him without knowing Him.

OSWALD CHAMBERS

WHO YOU KNOW

*Not everyone who calls out to me, "Lord! Lord!" will
enter the Kingdom of Heaven. Only those who actually
do the will of my Father in heaven will enter.*

MATTHEW 7:21

If the only people who get to enter heaven are those who
do the will of God, then who can qualify? Who does
God's will consistently?

Jesus tells of people who will proudly flash their religious credentials on Judgment Day. But when they reference their good works, Christ will reply, "I never knew
you" (Matthew 7:22-23).

It's knowing Jesus—period—that secures eternal life
for us (John 17:3). And knowing Jesus is only possible
through believing in him (John 6:68-69; 2 Timothy 1:12).

In short, heaven is about who you know, not what
you do.

*Salvation is worth working for. . . .
But we do not get it in that way.*

D. L. MOODY

DON'T BE A MISER

*The generous will prosper; those who refresh
others will themselves be refreshed.*

PROVERBS 11:25

Henrietta "Hetty" Green (1834–1916) is regarded as one
of the greatest misers of all time. Though her estate was
worth more than $100 million, she was known to conceal
her identity and seek free medical care. It is reported that
she refused to turn on the heat or use hot water, and she
sought to eat as cheaply as possible.

Stinginess is ugly, isn't it? Why stockpile assets that
you're just going to leave behind anyway?

Why not use your resources to bless others, trusting
that the infinite God, who gave you all those good things
in the first place, will continue to provide for your needs?

How will you show generosity today?

*If you own something you cannot give away,
then you don't own it, it owns you.*

ALBERT SCHWEITZER

THE TRUTH ABOUT GOD

*The LORD your God is indeed God. He is the
faithful God who keeps his covenant for a thousand
generations and lavishes his unfailing love on
those who love him and obey his commands.*

DEUTERONOMY 7:9

In our passage today, Moses looked out at the twelve tribes of Israel camped before him and reminded them of God's glorious character.

He urged them to take three great truths about God to heart: (1) he is the one true God; (2) he is faithful—we can trust him to keep every promise he makes; and (3) he is good—he pours out his love on those who walk with him.

You don't have to be camped on the plains of Moab to appreciate this great reminder. You serve the same God!

*People need to be reminded more often
than they need to be instructed.*

SAMUEL JOHNSON

NOVEMBER 15

GIVING CHEERFULLY

Remember this—a farmer who plants only a few seeds
will get a small crop. But the one who plants generously
will get a generous crop. You must each decide in your heart
how much to give. And don't give reluctantly or in response
to pressure. "For God loves a person who gives cheerfully."

2 CORINTHIANS 9:6-7

Paul's teaching in 2 Corinthians 8–9 is, perhaps, the most extensive passage on *giving* in the Bible. The thrust of these verses is "don't give grudgingly."

In short, if you don't want to give, don't. God certainly doesn't need your money.

But if you're unwilling to part with your cash, then ask yourself, "Why am I hesitating?" And pray, "Lord, make my heart generous, like yours."

How different our standard is from Christ's. We ask how
much a man gives. Christ asks how much he keeps.

ANDREW MURRAY

OUR SUN AND SHIELD

*The LORD God is our sun and our shield. He gives us
grace and glory. The LORD will withhold no
good thing from those who do what is right.*

PSALM 84:11

Lori's scared. Her future is dark, and the way forward
looks ominous. As a single mom with mounting bills and
a shaky job, she's feeling *extremely* vulnerable.

What she'd like is a miracle, of course. But until that
arrives, how about the promise of this verse? The psalmist
paints the picture of a God who shines on and surrounds
his people. He gives grace and glory abundantly when
life is grim and gritty.

We want the blueprint for the next five years. But
God says, "Take my hand. Let's just focus on doing the
next right thing."

*When a train goes through a tunnel and it
gets dark, you don't throw away the ticket and
jump off. You sit still and trust the engineer.*

CORRIE TEN BOOM

FIGHT FEAR WITH FAITH

When I am afraid, I will put my trust in you. I praise God for what he has promised. I trust in God, so why should I be afraid? What can mere mortals do to me?

PSALM 56:3-4

Fear confronts us in many forms: shy uneasiness—quietly whispering that something doesn't seem quite right; chatty anxiety—obnoxiously nagging and hounding us with every imaginable worst-case scenario; or traumatic terror—lunging out at us unexpectedly with petrifying effect.

Whatever fear looks like in your life today, David would say, "Meet it with faith. Even if you're shaking so hard you can't see straight, at least turn trembling to the one who has promised to be your Savior, Keeper, and Rock. Entrust yourself to him."

He that has his trust set upon God does not need to dread anything except the weakening or the paralysing of that trust.

ALEXANDER MACLAREN

THE FAITH TO DO NOTHING

*Be still in the presence of the LORD, and wait patiently
for him to act. Don't worry about evil people who
prosper or fret about their wicked schemes.*

PSALM 37:7

We typically think of heroic faith as "doing something."
You give sacrificially. You go somewhere hard and share
the gospel. You forgive an enemy. To be sure, such actions
do demonstrate great faith. But great faith is expressed
sometimes by doing nothing.

So often we instinctively rush in to fix things or
straighten people out or rescue a loved one from a mess.
But what if God wants us to let *him* be the Savior of
the world?

Sometimes the greatest display of faith is watching
and waiting, not working.

If you can't take time to do nothing, you're a slave to doing.

PETER KREEFT

NOVEMBER 19
NOT A GENIE

I tell you, you can pray for anything, and if you believe that you've received it, it will be yours.

MARK 11:24

Jesus is *not* saying in this verse, "I'll grant you any three wishes." He's a Savior, not a genie.

This is a command to pray with sincere faith. When we (or those we love) have legitimate needs, we should bring our requests to our heavenly Father, trusting that his heart is wise and good, and believing that "he rewards those who sincerely seek him" (Hebrews 11:6).

We must read promises that sound unconditional like this one alongside other biblical guidelines for prayer. God wants us to pray with great faith *and* according to his will (see Matthew 6:10), unselfishly (see James 4:3), and continually (see 1 Thessalonians 5:17).

Is this how *you* pray?

*He is the Giver not only of the answer,
but first of the prayer itself.*

P. T. FORSYTH

MONEY CAN'T BUY ME LOVE

Place me like a seal over your heart, like a seal on your arm. For love is as strong as death, its jealousy as enduring as the grave. Love flashes like fire, the brightest kind of flame. Many waters cannot quench love, nor can rivers drown it. If a man tried to buy love with all his wealth, his offer would be utterly scorned.

SONG OF SONGS 8:6-7

Today's world teaches that everything is for sale. According to Song of Songs, that simply isn't true. Love isn't for sale—it never has been.

If God has blessed you with romantic love, recognize that for the amazing gift that it is and don't take it for granted. Love is a supernatural gift that is stronger than death. Love flashes like fire, giving us a glimpse of the glory of God.

The word "romance," according to the dictionary, means excitement, adventure, and something extremely real. Romance should last a lifetime.

BILLY GRAHAM

ETERNAL WORD

In the beginning the Word already existed.
The Word was with God, and the Word was God.

JOHN 1:1

With one short sentence, John seized the attention of his first-century readers.

"In the beginning" reminded Jews of the opening chapters of Genesis (which describe the world's creation). The reference to "the Word" (the Greek word *logos*) reminded Greeks of their belief in a great governing principle that orders the universe.

John tapped into both ideas. He argued that this creative power or principle behind everything is a person—Jesus (John 1:14).

Put simply, Jesus is God. He made the world (see verse 3), then entered the world he made (see verse 10). Those who accept him become God's children (see verse 12).

Like all words, this "Word" revealed something—in this case, the very nature and person of God (see verse 18).

Amazing love! How can it be, that Thou,
my God, shouldst die for me?
CHARLES WESLEY

NOVEMBER 22

GOD, THE GREAT INITIATOR

---

*God showed his great love for us by sending Christ
to die for us while we were still sinners.*

ROMANS 5:8

Most religions take an "if-then" approach to salvation: "If you do _____, then God will do _____."

This puts humans in the driver's seat of salvation. We make the first move toward God—and hope to get his attention and win his favor.

The Christian faith declares a very different reality. The gospel says God is the initiator of salvation. He made the first move. When we were indifferent, even hostile, toward God, he sent Christ to die for us.

How much must he love us to do that while we were still sinners!

*Jesus sought me when a stranger, wandering
from the fold of God; he, to rescue me from
danger, bought me with his precious blood.*

ROBERT ROBINSON

NOVEMBER 23

MADE ALIVE

---

*You were dead because of your sins and because your
sinful nature was not yet cut away. Then God made
you alive with Christ, for he forgave all our sins.*

COLOSSIANS 2:13

The teaching of the Bible is that sin is a self-inflicted
disease that kills instantly, and that all people everywhere
are infected (Romans 3:23; 6:23). Apart from Christ, the
human race isn't just spiritually *sick* but spiritually *dead*.

The good news, Paul says, is that God in his grace
forgave all our sins and made us alive with Christ.

Here, Paul wants believers thinking of Jesus' lifeless
body in Joseph's tomb suddenly infused with the infinitely powerful life of God and rising from the dead.
What's more, he wants us seeing ourselves "with Christ,"
sharing in that same resurrection life today.

*Whatever man may do after regeneration, the first
quickening of the dead must originate with God.*

A. A. HODGE

WAGES AND GIFTS

*The wages of sin is death, but the free gift of God
is eternal life through Christ Jesus our Lord.*

ROMANS 6:23

If you have a job, you receive *wages*. Wages are payment, compensation, what you receive for work that you have done. If you have a fair and honest boss, wages are also what you deserve.

According to this famous verse, what we deserve from a just God in exchange for our sin is *death*—eternal separation from the one who is life itself.

But look at the rest of the verse. God has a free gift for us. Through Christ Jesus our Lord, God offers us eternal life. Our sin earned us death, but God offers us life instead.

Next time someone asks you what grace means, there's your answer.

*The doctrines of grace humble man without degrading
him, and exalt him without inflating him.*

CHARLES HODGE

NOVEMBER 25

PEACE WITH GOD

Since we have been made right in God's sight by
faith, we have peace with God because of what
Jesus Christ our Lord has done for us.

ROMANS 5:1

As he neared death, author Henry David Thoreau was asked by his aunt if he had made his peace with God. His famous reply? "I did not know that we had ever quarreled."

Someone needed to tell Thoreau that whether we quietly avoid God or aggressively shake our fists at him, we all "quarrel" with him. Sin is a defiant argument with our Creator. Worse, it's a war—either a shooting war or a cold war—against his rule.

Our hope for peace? Jesus! It's by trusting in his life, death, and resurrection that we are made right in God's sight.

Fallen man is not simply an imperfect creature who needs
improvement: he is a rebel who must lay down his arms.

C. S. LEWIS

EVERYTHING ELSE

Since he did not spare even his own Son but gave him
up for us all, won't he also give us everything else?

ROMANS 8:32

What do you need from God right now? What's the thing you sometimes struggle to believe that God will give? Joy? Peace of mind? Direction in life? Power over sin? The ability to forgive someone? A job? Healing in a certain relationship? Wisdom in raising children?

Paul's point is this: God has already demonstrated his infinite love for us in sending his own Son. If he willingly gave us his most precious gift, why wouldn't he give us lesser things?

If you have a need, don't be shy. Bring it to the Father, and trust his good and generous heart.

However many blessings we expect from God, His infinite
liberality will always exceed all our wishes and our thoughts.

JOHN CALVIN

NOVEMBER 27

NOT ASHAMED

I am not ashamed of this Good News about Christ.
It is the power of God at work, saving everyone who
believes—the Jew first and also the Gentile.

ROMANS 1:16

You get engaged, have a baby, or get a great new job. What do you do with such good news?

You feel embarrassed, right? Go into hiding and hope no one finds out, right? Wrong! You break speed records (and maybe even a leg) *rushing* to your smartphone to broadcast such news.

Likewise, when we experience the liberating truth of the gospel, it's not shame we feel. It's euphoria! We can't stop talking about what Jesus has done for us.

The gospel is powerful. It has the power to save people—but only when we speak it.

It is not our work to make men believe.
That is the work of the Holy Spirit.

D. L. MOODY

THE LORD'S PRESENCE IN CONFLICT

*Where two or three gather together as my
followers, I am there among them.*

MATTHEW 18:20

While discussing how to resolve conflicts and confront sin, Jesus mentioned the importance of believers praying together (Matthew 18:15-20)—and he seemed to promise his special presence in such gatherings.

To be sure, Christ is always "with" (Matthew 28:20) and "in" (Colossians 1:27) his followers. However, this verse is saying that when believers meet to discuss and pray about their differences (perhaps with a third party present to help referee), the Prince of Peace is present and eager to reconcile—because there's no better picture of the gospel than broken relationships restored by forgiveness that is both extended and received.

*It is the command of Jesus that none should come to the
altar with a heart that is unreconciled to his brother.*

DIETRICH BONHOEFFER

A DIFFERENT KIND OF LIST MAKING

*Let us think of ways to motivate one another
to acts of love and good works.*

HEBREWS 10:24

Are you a list maker (you know—tasks to do, stuff to buy, items to pack)?

Here, believers are urged to make a different kind of list: "ways to motivate one another to acts of love and good works."

This takes intentionality ("Let us think of ways"). Such pondering may produce a mental list, or one actually scribbled onto a notepad. Either way, considering how to spur others on is a hallmark of healthy families and spiritual communities.

Think about what you can say or do today to inspire those around you to make a difference. Pray that your community would do this for you, too.

*No one person can fulfill all your needs.
But the community can truly hold you.*

HENRI NOUWEN

THE GREAT ORCHESTRATOR

We know that God causes everything to work together for the good of those who love God and are called according to his purpose for them.

ROMANS 8:28

How good is God to those who love him and are called according to his purpose for them?

According to Paul, God is *this* good: believers can have absolute confidence ("we know") that the Almighty is in complete control of our lives ("God causes everything to work together for the good of those who love God").

This means God is able to redeem what's awful in our lives and weave together incidents that seem random and unrelated into a beautiful, unified story.

What in your current experience causes you to doubt this great promise? When have you experienced the truth of this promise?

Cheer up, Christian! Things are not left to chance: no blind fate rules the world. God hath purposes, and those purposes are fulfilled.

CHARLES H. SPURGEON

334

DIRTY WORDS?

*What is more pleasing to the LORD: your burnt
offerings and sacrifices or your obedience to his voice?
Listen! Obedience is better than sacrifice, and
submission is better than offering the fat of rams.*

1 SAMUEL 15:22

Surveys show that people are repulsed by the words *ooze,
pus, mucus, phlegm, maggots,* and *fester.* By the looks of
things, people aren't too crazy about the words *obedience*
and *submission* either.

Submission is listening and yielding to another.
Obedience is carrying out the wishes of a superior.

Here, the prophet Samuel tells the excuse-making
Saul that God wants us doing *his* will—not hiding our
disobedience under a flurry of religious activity.

To use a very unpopular word, are you fully *submitted*
to God today?

Obedience is the key to real faith.
CHARLES COLSON

DECEMBER 2

CLOSER

If it is true that you look favorably on me, let me
know your ways so I may understand you more fully
and continue to enjoy your favor. And remember
that this nation is your very own people.

EXODUS 33:13

This chapter of Exodus gives us a window to the remarkable relationship Moses enjoyed with God.

Though the two met often ("face to face, as one speaks to a friend," verse 11), Moses wasn't satisfied. He wanted more of God. Notice his passion to understand God more fully and to continue to enjoy God's favor (i.e., grace).

Moses' actions inspire questions to ask ourselves: *Is this my desire? When I get alone with God, am I merely seeking the things that God can give me, or do I want a more intimate knowledge of God himself?*

God is most glorified in us when we are most satisfied in him.

JOHN PIPER

TIME TO CHOOSE

If you refuse to serve the LORD, then choose today
whom you will serve. Would you prefer the gods your
ancestors served beyond the Euphrates? Or will it be the
gods of the Amorites in whose land you now live? But
as for me and my family, we will serve the LORD.

JOSHUA 24:15

Knowing his days were numbered, Joshua gathered the Israelites and asked them point blank: Are you going to serve the Lord or some false god?

Never mind that the Israelites had already pledged their devotion to God on *multiple* prior occasions. Spiritual commitment is like marriage. You make some initial promises, but then you have to decide to honor your vows on an ongoing basis.

Realize that you face the same spiritual choices today. How will you answer Joshua's question?

Now, just think a moment and answer the question,
"What shall I do with the Jesus who is called Christ?"

D. L. MOODY

GREAT QUESTIONS!

What do you benefit if you gain the whole world but lose your own soul? Is anything worth more than your soul?

MARK 8:36-37

An expert at asking great questions and a master storyteller, Jesus was the consummate teacher.

In this familiar passage, he was challenging his students (i.e., *disciples*) to give up petty, worldly ambitions and to give themselves fully to him.

In essence, he asked, "If I am who I say I am, and if this world isn't all there is, why not follow me gladly to a future that is truly out of this world? Why stockpile and salivate over temporal 'stuff' when it's your soul that's eternal?"

Put such questions to yourself: *Am I obsessing over worldly concerns? Consumed only with* now? *What if the world's definition of* winning *is actually* losing?

The water our souls require for survival is the assurance of salvation.

R. C. SPROUL

RADICAL

---

*If any of you wants to be my follower, you must give up
your own way, take up your cross daily, and follow me.*

LUKE 9:23

When crowds flocked to Jesus, he didn't try to win them
over with easy, breezy promises of worldly wealth and success. On the contrary, he stunned them by saying that following him requires the following: (1) Radical *repentance*
("give up your own way"). This means we stop pursuing
our own agendas and *our own* dreams and turn our desires
toward God's agenda. (2) Radical *commitment* ("take up
your cross daily"). This self-denial includes a willingness
to serve and even suffer, just as Jesus did. (3) Radical *per-
severance* ("follow me"). Followers *follow*—not once in a
while, but day in and day out.

Ask Jesus to give you a heart that says yes to all this.

*Christianity without discipleship is always
Christianity without Christ.*
DIETRICH BONHOEFFER

FALLING SHORT

*Everyone has sinned; we all fall short
of God's glorious standard.*

ROMANS 3:23

A holy God made humans to reflect his nature (Genesis 1:26-28). His desire for us? In Jesus' words: "Be perfect, even as your Father in heaven is perfect" (Matthew 5:48). That's the standard.

Sadly, in the holy bliss of Eden, Adam and Eve blatantly rejected God's authority. They looked elsewhere for life (which is the essence of sin). These two rebels then procreated an entire race of sinners.

We're all infected. We're all guilty. Sin has so warped our minds, wills, bodies, and spirits we can't *not* sin. We all fall short of God's glorious standard of holy perfection.

What to do? If your response is to drop to your knees in repentance, you're on the right track.

*Yea cannot slander human nature;
it is worse than words can paint it.*

CHARLES H. SPURGEON

SPIRITUAL SOAP

I confessed all my sins to you and stopped trying to hide
my guilt. I said to myself, "I will confess my rebellion to
the LORD." And you forgave me! All my guilt is gone.

PSALM 32:5

If after exercising, or a weekend campout, or working in
the yard all day you've been really dirty, smelly, and nasty,
then you know how wonderful a warm shower feels. That
clean, refreshing feeling is one of life's simple pleasures.

This is also true in a spiritual sense. Like David, when
we dive into the muck of sin, we need the cleansing that
comes from confessing our rebelliousness. Confession has
often been referred to as "the Christian's bar of soap."

If you've been giving in to sinful thoughts or actions,
let God shower you with his forgiveness and love.

The confession of evil works is the beginning of good works.
AUGUSTINE OF HIPPO

THE PROOF AND REWARDS OF LOVE

Those who accept my commandments and obey them are the ones who love me. And because they love me, my Father will love them. And I will love them and reveal myself to each of them.

JOHN 14:21

What's the clearest and simplest proof that a believer loves the Lord? (Hint: it's *not* powerful emotions felt during Sunday worship, a marked-up Bible, or that fish on your car.)

The correct answer is *obedience*.

Jesus made two things clear: (1) love *for* him and obedience *to* him are intertwined; and (2) loving submission brings tantalizing rewards—lovers of Jesus are promised a deeper experience of divine love. What's more, Jesus added, "And I will . . . reveal myself to each of them."

Obedience is love made visible.

Loving God—really loving Him—means living out His commands no matter what the cost.

CHARLES COLSON

WHAT A BLESSING!

May the LORD bless you and protect you.
May the LORD smile on you and be gracious to you.
May the LORD show you his favor and give you his peace.

NUMBERS 6:24-26

God gave this short benediction to his ancient priests, and it's no wonder some contemporary clergy still quote some form of it at the end of religious services.

Notice what this blessing reveals about God. His heart is to *bless*, which means he wants to give good things to his people in a covenant of loyal love. God wants to *protect* his people, to *smile* over and take pleasure in them, and to *show them favor* by lavishing them with his grace. Finally, the Lord wants to *give peace* to his people.

Remembering such truths about God's heart helps transform *our* hearts.

Satan does not here fill us with hatred of
God, but with forgetfulness of God.
DIETRICH BONHOEFFER

DON'T LET GO!

I cling to you; your strong right hand holds me securely.

PSALM 63:8

The child is so terrified, she literally has to be peeled off her father's leg. The driver on a mountain road is gripping the wheel so tightly, his knuckles turn white.

These are excellent pictures of what the psalmist means by "cling." This is the Hebrew "glue" word. It means "to stick to, to join, or to bind" oneself to someone or something. In fact, it's this word—"joined"—that is used in Genesis 2:24, the famous verse about marital oneness.

Here the psalmist, instead of giving in to despair or fear, grabs even more tightly to God. Clinging to the Almighty is wise. But what's much more important than our grip on him is his eternal grip on us.

To fear is to have more faith in your antagonist than in Christ.

D. L. MOODY

AFTER GOD'S OWN HEART

*Now your kingdom must end, for the LORD has
sought out a man after his own heart. The LORD has
already appointed him to be the leader of his people,
because you have not kept the LORD's command.*

1 SAMUEL 13:14

David's epic life earned him multiple nicknames. Those who remember his defeat of Goliath label him the "giant slayer." Scholars speak of the "shepherd-king" of Israel. David called himself "the sweet psalmist of Israel" (2 Samuel 23:1). The prophet Samuel referred to him interestingly as "a man after [God's] own heart."

To be after God's own heart means to hunger to know God and do his will. As David's roller-coaster life shows, even when we disobey God, we can return to him in faith and he will always restore us.

Resolution One: I will live for God.
Resolution Two: If no one else does, I still will.

JONATHAN EDWARDS

COVETING OR CONTENTMENT?

I have learned how to be content with whatever I have.

PHILIPPIANS 4:11

The apostle Paul faced some difficult circumstances in his life and ministry. But whether he was facing feast or famine, he recognized that God was in control and that God would provide. And so Paul chose to be content.

We are frequently faced with situations that offer us two choices: coveting or contentment. We can choose to want what others have, or we can be content with what God has given us.

The cure for coveting is to cultivate a spirit of contentment. Ask God to help you learn to be grateful for what you do have, instead of fixating on what you don't.

He who is able to accept everything gladly from the Lord—including darkness, dryness, flatness—and completely disregard self is he who lives for Him.

WATCHMAN NEE

GOD'S SEARCH

The LORD God called to the man, "Where are you?"

GENESIS 3:9

This might be the saddest and—simultaneously—most encouraging verse in all the Bible.

The moment Adam and Eve disobeyed the Lord God in Eden, they were overwhelmed by shame. Hearing the approach of the Lord, they dove into the bushes where they cowered in fear and trembled with guilt. And frankly, that's been the sad behavior of the human race ever since—running and hiding from God.

But notice God's encouraging response to them. He comes. He searches. He calls. His question is not really about getting information. It's an invitation: "Come out of hiding. Let's get you healed."

And thousands of years after this first rebellion, Christmas is the ultimate picture of God's search for his wayward children.

The more you think about it, the more staggering it gets. Nothing in fiction is so fantastic as is this truth of the Incarnation.

J. I. PACKER

DECEMBER 14

THE INFINITE INFANT

All right then, the Lord himself will give you the sign. Look!
The virgin will conceive a child! She will give birth to a son
and will call him Immanuel (which means "God is with us").

ISAIAH 7:14

One by one, the players get clues. With furrowed brows, they take turns guessing what it all means. Only later, after the answer is revealed, do all the hints make sense.

This is how Old Testament prophecies (like this verse) work. God was hinting, gradually unveiling his "answer" to the world: "Get ready! I'm coming for a visit! Watch for a pregnant virgin."

No wonder C. S. Lewis called the Incarnation "the central event in the history of the Earth." All of salvation history had been leading to that moment.

We must never allow anything to blind us to the true
significance of what happened at Bethlehem so long ago.
Nothing can alter the fact that we live on a visited planet.

J. B. PHILLIPS

THE ULTIMATE GIFT

*A child is born to us, a son is given to us. The government
will rest on his shoulders. And he will be called: Wonderful
Counselor, Mighty God, Everlasting Father, Prince of Peace.*

ISAIAH 9:6

Christmas shopping tip #1: the presents you wish you
had most, and the gifts you'd most like to give your loved
ones, can't be bought online or in a store at all.

What are the big needs? Guidance in decision making? Strength to face whatever life throws at us? A secure
confidence that we are forever loved? A deep, abiding
sense that all is well?

Read Isaiah's beloved prophecy again. We find all
these blessings in God's gift of a child, not at the mall.

Maybe this season we'd be wise to do more praying
and less shopping.

*Christmas is fast approaching. And now that Christ has
aroused our seasonal expectations, he'll soon fulfill them all!*

AUGUSTINE OF HIPPO

SAVING FAITH

If you openly declare that Jesus is Lord and believe in your heart that God raised him from the dead, you will be saved.

ROMANS 10:9

James, the half brother of Jesus, wrote about a faith that cannot save (James 2:19). This kind of intellectual agreement nods at theological statements about the existence of God, admits, "Yep, that's true," and continues on its way unchanged. James says that even demons, who will not be saved, believe that God exists.

Paul emphasizes heart-level belief. It's more than merely thinking and talking about spiritual ideas. It's trusting—in the core of our being—that Jesus is Lord, he was crucified for our sin, and he was raised to give us new life.

Which kind of faith do you have?

It is not great faith, but true faith, that saves; and the salvation lies not in the faith, but in the Christ in whom faith trusts.

CHARLES H. SPURGEON

HUMILITY, NOT
SELF-PROMOTION

*Those who exalt themselves will be humbled, and
those who humble themselves will be exalted.*

MATTHEW 23:12

Should you ever decide to offer a product or service to the world, you'll encounter hundreds of marketers and social media gurus telling you to "Get your name out there! Build your brand! Grow your platform!"

Translation? "Use my surefire gimmicks—only $39.95—to gain thousands of followers on social media."

While there is certainly business wisdom in letting people know about what you can offer, there's also a dark side to all this self-promotion. We can become self-absorbed, oblivious to others, and overly reliant on our own abilities.

God frowns when we try to make our names great without his elevating us (Genesis 11:4). He wants us faithfully trusting him and humbly allowing him to bless us (Genesis 12:2).

Real true faith is man's weakness leaning on God's strength.

D. L. MOODY

MIRACLE BABY

*Mary asked the angel, "But how can this happen?
I am a virgin." The angel replied, "The Holy Spirit
will come upon you, and the power of the Most High
will overshadow you. So the baby to be born will
be holy, and he will be called the Son of God."*

LUKE 1:34-35

The Apostles' Creed declares that Jesus "was conceived
by the Holy Spirit, born of the Virgin Mary." This means
Jesus had a divine Father and a human mother. He was
and is both God and man.

A mystery? Absolutely. A miracle? Yes. Theological
trivia? No way. Only a human could represent sinners,
and only a God could rescue them.

The Virgin Birth is essential to our faith.

*The life of Jesus is bracketed by two impossibilities:
a virgin's womb and an empty tomb. Jesus entered
our world through a door marked "No Entrance,"
and left through a door marked "No Exit."*

PETER LARSON

HOW TO ANSWER AN ANGEL

Mary responded, "I am the Lord's servant.
May everything you have said about me come
true." And then the angel left her.

LUKE 1:38

Some Christians come close to worshiping Mary. Others are guilty of ignoring her remarkable life. So what's the right approach? To appreciate—and emulate—her amazing devotion to God.

Nowhere is Mary's commitment clearer than in this familiar moment when the angel Gabriel has just announced the startling news that she, an unmarried teenager, has been chosen to be the mother of the Messiah.

Almost overcome by shock and awe, Mary acquiesces, managing to whisper, "I am the Lord's servant."

It's this kind of spirit that makes for a truly meaningful Christmas.

This attitude of complete submission and complete trust is of
course the key to working out our own salvation in fear and
trembling and is the mark of a truly spiritual Christian.

JOHN F. WALVOORD

SEEING GOD!

Christ is the visible image of the invisible God. He existed before anything was created and is supreme over all creation.

COLOSSIANS 1:15

After the epic question "Is there a God?" humanity's next most fundamental question is "What is God like?"

Paul answers both questions in one verse when he says, "Christ is the visible image of the invisible God." Another translation for the word *image* could be "icon." So one could say that Christ is the "icon" of God. In other words, Jesus is a living portrait or picture of God. In Jesus' own words, "Anyone who has seen me has seen the Father!" (John 14:9).

Moses, Buddha, Confucius, Muhammad—history is full of influential religious leaders. But only one—Jesus— perfectly resembles and reveals God's character and nature. Jesus is God incarnate. Only he deserves our devotion.

He [Jesus] will reign over you, either by your own consent, or without it.

CHARLES H. SPURGEON

NAME ABOVE ALL NAMES

She will have a son, and you are to name him Jesus,
for he will save his people from their sins.

MATTHEW 1:21

Of all the names in the Bible, including famous ones like
Abraham, Moses, David, and *Paul,* one name stands apart
from and above all the rest—*Jesus.*

Jesus is the Greek form of the Hebrew name *Joshua.* It
means "the LORD is salvation." It was actually a common
name during that time period in that culture. For many
parents, bestowing this name was a kind of prayer, asking
God to save his people.

In this particular infant, the people of Israel—and the
world—finally got the answer to all those prayers.

Hark! The herald angels sing, "Glory to the newborn King;
peace on earth and mercy mild, God and sinners reconciled!"

CHARLES WESLEY

THE BIRTH

*She gave birth to her firstborn son. She wrapped him
snugly in strips of cloth and laid him in a manger,
because there was no lodging available for them.*

LUKE 2:7

No matter how many times we hear it, this story never
gets old.

The couple making the best of a challenging situation—
finding a suitable place for the delivery; the child's arrival;
the baby cradled in the place near where livestock slurped
up their food.

There are so many details Luke omits: Was it a cold
night? Was there a cruel innkeeper? Were they in a stable
or a cave? Were they alone?

Maybe in the end, the only detail that really matters
is that Jesus did, in fact, come.

*The Word of God, Jesus Christ, on account of
his great love for mankind, became what we are
in order to make us what he is himself.*

IRENAEUS

GOOD NEWS, GREAT JOY

*The angel reassured them. "Don't be afraid!" he said.
"I bring you good news that will bring great joy to all
people. The Savior—yes, the Messiah, the Lord—has
been born today in Bethlehem, the city of David!"*

LUKE 2:10-11

Surely, there must have been other children born that night. But none generated heavenly fanfare like this.

A great army of angels was dispatched, not to the royal palace or the Temple in Jerusalem, but to a field where a motley group of shepherds were caring for their flocks of sheep.

They sat in stunned silence—until the angels departed. Then they left too, making a mad dash to find the baby—which, when you think about it, is really the only kind of *dashing* that befits the season.

Joy to the world, the Lord is come! Let earth receive her King!

ISAAC WATTS

WHAT TO GIVE A KING

---

*They entered the house and saw the child with his
mother, Mary, and they bowed down and worshiped
him. Then they opened their treasure chests and
gave him gifts of gold, frankincense, and myrrh.*

MATTHEW 2:11

Much of what we think about the wise men is hazy legend,
not biblical fact.

Matthew places them at the house to see the child
(not at the manger to visit the baby). We assume there
were three (because of the three gifts). There may have
been two or five or fourteen. Did they ride camels? The
Bible doesn't say.

What isn't foggy is the magi's devotion. They gave
Jesus their time, effort, worship, and treasure—all worthy
gifts for a King.

*The Magi didn't return to the Orient by the same
route they arrived on. Learn from the past. If you
want to change your life, then change your way.*

AUGUSTINE OF HIPPO

THE UNOPENED GIFT

I am leaving you with a gift—peace of mind
and heart. And the peace I give is a gift the world
cannot give. So don't be troubled or afraid.

JOHN 14:27

A. W. Tozer observed sadly, "Christ came to bring peace and we celebrate His coming by making peace impossible for six weeks of each year."

How tragic. With such emphasis on *gifts* at this time of year, how is it that we fail to open (and enjoy) the Lord's remarkable gift of *peace*?

The Hebrew word for "peace" is *shalom*. Shalom isn't just a quiet house when extended family leaves and the kids get back in school. Shalom is the deep conviction that Jesus is Lord and his Word is true.

Is peace the one Christmas gift you still haven't opened?

Peace comes when we are assured that there is no earth-born
cloud between our lives and God. Peace is the consequence
of forgiveness, which in turn is God's removal of that which
hides or obscures His face, and breaks union with Him.

CHARLES H. BRENT

BACK TO NORMAL?

The Word became human and made his home among us.
He was full of unfailing love and faithfulness. And we have
seen his glory, the glory of the Father's one and only Son.

JOHN 1:14

For many, December looks like this: weeks one and two
are filled with excitement and anticipation. Weeks three
and four are marked by exhaustion and frustration.

All that shopping and cooking and decorating, all
the parties and traveling and house guests—it grinds us
down. The big day can't come and go soon enough. We
just want our lives back. We just want to get back to
normal.

But here's the thing: because of what Advent means,
nothing can ever be "normal" again.

God came to us in Christ. And he is coming again!

Veiled in flesh, the Godhead see; hail the incarnate Deity.
Pleased as man with men to dwell, Jesus, our Emmanuel.

CHARLES WESLEY

STANDING AT GOD'S THRONE

I saw a vast crowd, too great to count, from every nation and tribe and people and language, standing in front of the throne and before the Lamb. They were clothed in white robes and held palm branches in their hands.

REVELATION 7:9

How terrible is prejudice and racial animosity?

The beginning of the Bible indicates that we humans *all* share a common ancestry.

The middle of the Bible says that *all* races and people groups share a common problem (sin) and a common need (forgiveness). Thankfully, we also share a common Savior (Jesus).

The end of the Bible reveals that *all* those who trust and follow Jesus will end up around the throne of God, living eternally for his glory.

So why would we treat one another with anything less than love and respect?

He rules the world with truth and grace.

ISAAC WATTS

CHIP AWAY

The master was full of praise. "Well done, my good and
faithful servant. You have been faithful in handling
this small amount, so now I will give you many
more responsibilities. Let's celebrate together!"

MATTHEW 25:21

As we draw near the close of another year, perhaps you're prone to look back wistfully and think, "Why didn't I
_____?"

Stop. Quit berating yourself over missed opportunities. Open your eyes to the possibilities of *this* day, and—Lord willing—the new year that stretches out in front of you.

We long to do grandiose things. But God wants us chipping away faithfully at the small things he puts in our path each day. That's how we build a life that pleases God.

What are two simple things you can do for God's glory *today*?

If you can't fly, run. If you can't run, walk. If you
can't walk, crawl, but by all means, keep moving.

MARTIN LUTHER KING JR.

EVERYTHING NEW

He will wipe every tear from their eyes, and there will be no
more death or sorrow or crying or pain. All these things are
gone forever. And the one sitting on the throne said, "Look,
I am making everything new!" And then he said to me,
"Write this down, for what I tell you is trustworthy and true."

REVELATION 21:4-5

The book of Revelation—the apostle John's eye-popping
peek into the future—often leaves us scratching our
heads. At least *this* particular scene isn't hard to interpret.

The day is coming when the curtain will come down
on our broken, suffering world. God himself will wipe
every tear from our eyes! Then, he will remake everything.

As promises go, these ones are enough to get our
hearts racing with anticipation.

Christianity . . . provides a unified
answer for the whole of life.
FRANCIS A. SCHAEFFER

DECEMBER 30

SOUL TALK

Why am I discouraged? Why is my heart so
sad? I will put my hope in God! I will praise
him again—my Savior and my God!

PSALM 42:11

When trouble strikes, it's easy to react by making a flurry
of bad decisions. This is why this verse is so beloved.
Look at all the things the psalmist does right:

He names what he's feeling ("discouraged," "sad").
He questions—even calls out—his own soul ("Why . . .
why?"). He forcefully speaks his intentions ("I will . . .
I will"). He calls on the one who can deliver him ("my
Savior and my God").

The good news? Every believer can do these things!

The Lord's mercy often rides to the door of our hearts on the
black horse of affliction. Jesus uses the whole range of our
experience to wean us from earth and woo us to Heaven.

CHARLES H. SPURGEON

THE GREAT REALIZATION

*Be still, and know that I am God! I will be honored by
every nation. I will be honored throughout the world.*

PSALM 46:10

We hurtle from one thing to another, constantly lamenting our crazy schedules. (Never mind the truth that *we* control our schedules.) No wonder we're so frantic in the present, so nervous about the future.

To all our feverish scrambling, God says, "Quiet! Let go. Relax. I'm the Almighty. Nothing in this world is out of my control. Everything—including your life—is on track, and all will be well."

It would do us good to quiet our souls daily and think on such things as we get ready to begin a new year.

*We are so afraid of silence that we chase ourselves
from one event to the next in order not to have
to spend a moment alone with ourselves, in order
not to have to look at ourselves in the mirror.*

DIETRICH BONHOEFFER

Do-able. _Daily._ Devotions.

START ANY DAY THE ONE YEAR WAY.

For Women

_The One Year®
Home and
Garden
Devotions_

_The One Year®
Devotions for
Women_

_The One Year®
Devotions for
Moms_

_The One Year®
Women of the
Bible_

_The One Year®
Coffee with God_

_The One Year®
Devotional of Joy
and Laughter_

_The One Year®
Women's
Friendship
Devotional_

_The One Year®
Wisdom
for Women
Devotional_

_The One Year®
Book of Amish
Peace_

_The One Year®
Women in
Christian History
Devotional_

For Men

*The One Year®
Devotions for
Men on the Go*

*The One Year®
Devotions for Men*

*The One Year®
Father-Daughter
Devotions*

For Families

*The One Year®
Family
Devotions, Vol. 1*

*The One Year®
Dinner Table
Devotions*

For Couples

*The One Year®
Devotions for
Couples*

*The One Year® Love
Language Minute
Devotional*

*The One Year® Love
Talk Devotional*

For Teens

*The One Year®
Devos for Teens*

*The One Year®
Be-Tween You
and God*

For Personal Growth

*The One Year®
at His Feet
Devotional*

*The One Year®
Uncommon Life
Daily Challenge*

*The One Year®
Recovery Prayer
Devotional*

*The One Year®
Christian History*

*The One Year®
Experiencing God's
Presence Devotional*

For Bible Study

*The One Year®
Praying through
the Bible*

*The One Year®
Praying the
Promises of God*

*The One Year®
Through the
Bible Devotional*

*The One Year®
Book of Bible
Promises*

*The One Year®
Unlocking the
Bible Devotional*

TheOneYear.com

CP0145